Women in the Old Testament
Part Two

Women in the Old Testament
Part Two

Irene Nowell, OSB

with **Jaime L. Waters**

and Little Rock Scripture Study staff

Little Rock
Scripture Study

LITURGICAL PRESS
Collegeville, Minnesota

littlerockscripture.org

Nihil obstat for the commentary text by Irene Nowell: Reverend Robert Harren, *Censor deputatus.*
Imprimatur for the commentary text by Irene Nowell: ✠ Most Reverend John F. Kinney, J.C.D., D.D., Bishop of Saint Cloud, Minnesota, April 9, 2010.

Cover design by John Vineyard. Interior art by Ned Bustard. Photos and illustrations on pages 16, 22, 24, 41, 43, 61, 63, 70, 86, and 93 courtesy of Getty Images.

 This symbol indicates material that was created by Little Rock Scripture Study to supplement the biblical text and commentary. Some of these inserts first appeared in the *Little Rock Catholic Study Bible*; others were created specifically for this book by Catherine Upchurch.

1   2   3   4   5   6   7   8   9

Library of Congress Cataloging-in-Publication Data

Names: Nowell, Irene, 1940– author. | Waters, Jaime L., author. | Little Rock Scripture Study Staff, author.
Title: Women in the Old Testament / Irene Nowell, OSB, Jaime L. Waters and Little Rock Scripture Study Staff.
Description: Collegeville, [Minnesota] : Liturgical Press, 2024. | Series: Little Rock scripture study | Summary: "Women in the Old Testament explores Israel's beginnings, Israel's captivity and freedom, and Israel's tribal period from the perspective of the earliest women of salvation history, such as Sarah, Deborah, Ruth, Judith, and Esther. Includes classic commentary by Irene Nowell, OSB and contemporary scholarship by Jaime Waters. Study and reflection questions, prayers, and access to online lectures also included"— Provided by publisher.
Identifiers: LCCN 2024002658 (print) | LCCN 2024002659 (ebook) | ISBN 9780814668375 (v. 1 ; trade paperback) | ISBN 9780814668405 (v. 2 ; trade paperback) | ISBN 9780814668399 (v. 1 ; ebook) | ISBN 9780814668429 (v. 2 ; ebook)
Subjects: LCSH: Women in the Bible. | Bible Ole Testament | BISAC: RELIGION / Biblical Commentary / Old Testament / Prophets | RELIGION / Christianity / Catholic
Classification: LCC BS575 .N64 2024 (print) | LCC BS575 (ebook) | DDC 221.9/22082—dc23/eng/20240321
LC record available at https://lccn.loc.gov/2024002658
LC ebook record available at https://lccn.loc.gov/2024002659

TABLE OF CONTENTS

Wrap-Up Lectures and Discussion Tips for Facilitators are available for each lesson at no charge. Find them online at LittleRockScripture.org/Lectures/WomenOTPartTwo.

Welcome

The Bible is at the heart of what it means to be a Christian. It is the Spirit-inspired word of God for us. It reveals to us the God who created, redeemed, and guides us still. It speaks to us personally and as a church. It forms the basis of our public liturgical life and our private prayer lives. It urges us to live worthily and justly, to love tenderly and wholeheartedly, and to be a part of building God's kingdom here on earth.

Though it was written a long time ago, in the context of a very different culture, the Bible is no relic of the past. Catholic biblical scholarship is among the best in the world, and in our time and place, we have unprecedented access to it. By making use of solid scholarship, we can discover much about the ancient culture and religious practices that shaped those who wrote the various books of the Bible. With these insights, and by praying with the words of Scripture, we allow the words and images to shape us as disciples. By sharing our journey of faithful listening to God's word with others, we have the opportunity to be stretched in our understanding and to form communities of love and learning. Ultimately, studying and praying with God's word deepens our relationship with Christ.

Women in the Old Testament, Part Two

The resource you hold in your hands is divided into four lessons. Each lesson involves personal prayer and study using this book and the experience of group prayer, discussion, and wrap-up lecture.

If you are using this resource in the context of a small group, we suggest that you meet four times, discussing one lesson per meeting. Allow about 90 minutes for the small group gathering. Small groups function best with eight to twelve people to ensure good group dynamics and to allow all to participate as they wish.

Some groups choose to have an initial gathering before their regular sessions begin. This allows an opportunity to meet one another, pass out books, and, if desired, view the optional intro lecture for this study available on the "Resources" page of the Little Rock Scripture Study website (littlerockscripture.org). Please note that there is only one intro lecture for two-part studies.

Every Bible study group is a little bit different. Some of our groups like to break each lesson up into two weeks of study so they are reading less each week and have more time to discuss the questions together at their weekly gatherings. If your group wishes to do this, simply agree how much of each lesson will be read each week, and only answer the questions that correspond to the material you read. Wrap-up lectures can then be viewed at the end of every other meeting rather than at the end of every meeting. Of course, this will mean that your study will last longer, and your group will meet more times.

WHAT MATERIALS WILL YOU USE?

The materials in this book include:

- Scripture passages to be studied, using the New American Bible Revised Edition as the translation.
- Commentary by Irene Nowell, with introduction, updates, and essays by Jaime L. Waters.
- Occasional inserts ⬢ highlighting elements of the Scripture passages being studied. Some of these appear also in the *Little Rock Catholic Study Bible* while others are supplied by staff writers.
- Questions for study, reflection, and discussion at the end of each lesson.
- Opening and closing prayers for each lesson, as well as other prayer forms available in the closing pages of the book.

In addition, there are wrap-up lectures available for each lesson. Your group may choose to purchase a DVD containing these lectures or make use of the video lectures available online at no charge. The link to these free lectures is: LittleRockScripture.org/Lectures/WomenOTPartTwo. Of course, if your group has access to qualified speakers, you may choose to have live presentations.

Each person will need a current translation of the Bible. We recommend the *Little Rock Catholic Study Bible*, which makes use of the New American Bible Revised Edition. Other translations, such as the New Jerusalem Bible or the New Revised Standard Version Updated Edition, would also work well.

HOW WILL YOU USE THESE MATERIALS?

Prepare in advance

Using Lesson One as an example:

- Begin with a simple prayer like the one found on page 11.

- Read the assigned material for Lesson One (pages 12–33) so that you are prepared for the weekly small group session.
- Answer the questions, Exploring Lesson One, found at the end of the assigned reading, pages 34–36.
- Use the Closing Prayer on page 36 when you complete your study. This prayer may be used again when you meet with the group.

Meet with your small group

- After introductions and greetings, allow time for prayer (about 5 minutes) as you begin the group session. You may use the prayer on page 11 (also used by individuals in their preparation) or use a prayer of your choosing.
- Spend about 45–50 minutes discussing the responses to the questions that were prepared in advance. You may also develop your discussion further by responding to questions and interests that arise during the discussion and faith-sharing itself.
- Close the discussion and faith-sharing with prayer, about 5–10 minutes. You may use the Closing Prayer at the end of each lesson or one of your choosing at the end of the book. It is important to allow people to pray for personal and community needs and to give thanks for how God is moving in your lives.
- Listen to or view the wrap-up lecture associated with each lesson (10–15 minutes). You may watch the lecture online, use a DVD, or provide a live lecture by a qualified local speaker. View the lecture together at the end of the session or, if your group runs out of time, you may invite group members to watch the lecture on their own time after the discussion.

A note to individuals

- If you are using this resource for individual study, simply move at your own pace. Take as much time as you need to read, study, and pray with the material.
- If you would like to share this experience with others, consider inviting a friend or family member to join you for your next study. Even a small group of two or three provides an opportunity for fruitful dialog and faith-sharing!

Women in the Old Testament

Part Two

LESSON ONE

Introduction and
Women of Israel's Monarchy

Begin your personal study and group discussion with a simple and sincere prayer such as:

Prayer

You, O God, fill your people with courage, wisdom, and humility. Inspire us, as you inspired the women of Scripture, to use these virtues to transform the world.

Read the Introduction and pages 14–33, Lesson One.

Respond to the questions on pages 34–36, Exploring Lesson One.

The Closing Prayer on page 36 is for your personal use and may be used at the end of group discussion.

INTRODUCTION

Part Two of *Women in the Old Testament* by Irene Nowell, OSB, builds on the content covered in Part One, shifting the focus to biblical women after the development of the Israelite monarchy. Eve and Woman Wisdom are also considered in a lesson focused especially on the image of God. Like Part One of this study, Part Two maintains the spirit, interests, and vast majority of Irene Nowell's original work.

Features of this Edition

In completing the updates to *Women in the Old Testament* for this Little Rock Scripture Study edition, I have been attentive to Nowell's style, content, and organization, revising only as needed while relying on my own background as a contemporary scholar of the Old Testament and my particular teaching and research interests in the areas of women in Scripture as well as feminist and womanist biblical criticism. Some language and content have been edited, updated, or adjusted in light of developments in biblical scholarship. For example, biblical scholarship today tends to be more cautious when making assertions about dating texts and text sources. Likewise, revisions to *Women in the Old Testament* have been attentive to the language used in discussing biblical women, updating as needed in a contemporary context. The biblical text in this edition has also been updated to follow the New American Bible Revised Edition (NABRE).

A significant change in this new edition of *Women in the Old Testament* is the addition of "Continuing the Conversation" sections at the end of each lesson. Here I have offered supplementary details, new perspectives, or further discussion of biblical characters or themes. This new content is designed to enrich your reflection on women in the Old Testament, expand upon Nowell's interpretations, and add another voice to the ongoing conversation about biblical women. It is my hope that these sections will spark conversation within your small groups

and provide opportunities for you to add your own voices to contemporary conversations about women in Scripture, in society, and in our church.

Briefer essays entitled "More Women of the Old Testament" can also be found throughout the study. Here I've provided a bit of information about other notable women of the Old Testament that you may find interesting. In addition to these essays, you'll find informative inserts, indicated by a flame symbol, that are excerpted from the *Little Rock Catholic Study Bible* or written specifically for this study by Catherine Upchurch. At the end of each lesson, questions will help you reflect on and discuss what you've learned, and prayers will help you pray with the biblical texts and with your group.

The Women You Will Study

Part Two consists of four lessons. Lesson One explores women in the books of Samuel and Kings. In 1 and 2 Samuel, Michal, Bathsheba, and Tamar (not to be confused with the Tamar of Gen 38) are highlighted as significant women in the early stages of the monarchy. Each of these women is connected to King David as a wife (Michal, Bathsheba) or daughter (Tamar). Royal women from outside of Israel are also highlighted in this lesson, such as the queen of Sheba and Jezebel (a Phoenician princess who becomes queen of Israel). Lesson Two focuses on the theme of women created in the image of God. Eve in the book of Genesis is highlighted. In addition, Woman Wisdom as an image of God is explored in the books of Proverbs, Sirach, and the Wisdom of Solomon. Lesson Three examines the courage and strength of Judith and Susanna, women who are featured in the deuterocanonical material of the Old Testament. These traditions are from the Greek translation of the Old Testament (known as the Septuagint). Finally, Lesson Four is devoted to the book of Esther, describing the biblical traditions about Queens Vashti and Esther, whose stories are set during the period of Persian rule.

Each lesson examines a group of women, unpacking the main elements of their stories and, when relevant, how they interact with other women in the texts. The ways that women interact with, affect, or are affected by men are also significant aspects of these studies. In exploring biblical women, these lessons show the complexities and struggles that life in antiquity might have entailed. The important roles women played in their families, communities, and in advancing salvation history are highlighted. These lessons also consider different historical settings and literary depictions of women. You will have opportunities to reflect on the actions of women in different contexts, the presence of God in their stories, and the ways biblical women might inspire faith and theological reflection in our lives today.

I invite you to embark on this journey with an open heart and mind as you encounter God through women in the Old Testament. It is my hope that these lessons will provide intellectually and spiritually stimulating ways to engage with these important Scripture texts.

—Jaime L. Waters

WOMEN OF ISRAEL'S MONARCHY

Scripture excerpts are found in shaded text boxes throughout the lesson. For additional context, you may wish to read all of the following in your Bible: 1 Samuel 18:20–19:17; 2 Samuel 3:6-30; 6:1-23; 11:1–12:25; 13:1-22; 1 Kings 1:1–2:25; 10:1-13; 16:29-33; 18–19; 21; 2 Kings 9.

Israel's era of judges and tribes eventually gives way to a centralized monarchy, a situation that leads to its own political, social, and religious challenges. The women surrounding David and his kingship are for the most part at the mercy of his whims and power, while one later queen rises to wield her own influence in Israel.

MICHAL

The Bride

1 Samuel 18:20-29

20Now Saul's daughter Michal loved David. When this was reported to Saul, he was pleased. 21He thought, "I will offer her to him as a trap, so that the hand of the Philistines may strike him." So for the second time Saul said to David, "You shall become my son-in-law today." 22Saul then ordered his servants, "Speak to David privately and say: The king favors you, and all his officers love you. You should become son-in-law to the king." 23But when Saul's servants mentioned this to David, he said: "Is becoming the king's son-in-law a trivial matter in your eyes? I am poor and insignificant." 24When his servants reported David's answer to him, 25Saul commanded them, "Say this to David: The king desires no other price for the bride than the foreskins of one hundred Philistines, that he may thus take vengeance on his enemies." Saul intended to have David fall into the hands of the Philistines. 26When the servants reported this offer to David, he was pleased with the prospect of becoming the king's son-in-law. Before the year was up, 27David arose and went with his men and slew two hundred Philistines. He brought back their foreskins and counted them out before the king that he might become the king's son-in-law. So Saul gave him his daughter Michal as wife. 28Then Saul realized that the LORD was with David and that his own daughter Michal loved David. 29So Saul feared David all the more and was his enemy ever after.

Saul, Israel's first king, had three sons and two daughters. The younger daughter is named Michal (1 Sam 14:49). Michal's story is framed by two sentences: "Saul's daughter Michal loved David" (1 Sam 18:20) and "Michal, daughter of Saul, . . . despised [David] in her heart" (2 Sam 6:16). Throughout her story she is used as a pawn by men seeking power.

In the beginning Michal loves David. Saul, seeing this, decides to use her to eliminate David. He offers her to David at the bride-price of one hundred Philistine foreskins. David must kill one hundred enemy men and return the evidence to the king. Saul hopes that the Philistines will kill David. Instead, David returns to Saul with evidence that he has killed two hundred Philistines. Saul's ploy does not work. Michal is given to David in marriage. She loves him; nowhere does the text tell us if he loves her.

1 Samuel 19:11-17

[11]The same night, Saul sent messengers to David's house to guard it, planning to kill him in the morning. David's wife Michal informed him, "Unless you run for your life tonight, tomorrow you will be killed." [12]Then Michal let David down through a window, and he made his escape in safety. [13]Michal took the teraphim and laid it in the bed, putting a tangle of goat's hair at its head and covering it with a blanket. [14]When Saul sent officers to arrest David, she said, "He is sick." [15]Saul, however, sent the officers back to see David and commanded them, "Bring him up to me in his bed, that I may kill him." [16]But when the messengers entered, they found the teraphim in the bed, with the tangle of goat's hair at its head. [17]Saul asked Michal: "Why did you lie to me like this? You have helped my enemy to get away!" Michal explained to Saul: "He threatened me, saying 'Let me go or I will kill you.'"

More Women of the Old Testament

The Prophet Huldah

The female prophet Huldah, identified in 2 Kings 22 as the wife of Shallum, "keeper of the [royal] wardrobe," sparks a period of reform associated with King Josiah. During Josiah's reign, the high priest Hilkiah finds the book of the law (a portion of the book of Deuteronomy) in the temple. The book is read to Josiah, who grieves and repents for Israel's disregard for the law. In response to Josiah's request that God be consulted about the book, Hilkiah and other royal officials go to Huldah, which shows her proximity and prominence in the royal court. Huldah then issues the longest prophetic message by a woman in the Old Testament:

> [S]he said to them, "Thus says the LORD, the God of Israel: Say to the man who sent you to me, Thus says the LORD: I am about to bring evil upon this place and upon its inhabitants—all the words of the book which the king of Judah has read. Because they have abandoned me and have burned incense to other gods, provoking me by all the works of their hands, my rage is ablaze against this place and it cannot be extinguished. But to the king of Judah who sent you to consult the LORD, give this response: Thus says the LORD, the God of Israel: As for the words you have heard, because you were heartsick and have humbled yourself before the LORD when you heard what I have spoken concerning this place and its inhabitants, that they would become a desolation and a curse; and because you tore your garments and wept before me, I in turn have heard, oracle of the LORD. I will therefore gather you to your ancestors; you shall go to your grave in peace, and your eyes shall not see all the evil I am about to bring upon this place." This they reported to the king. (2 Kgs 22:15-20)

As a result of Huldah's prophecy, Josiah begins to aggressively dismantle unsanctioned cultic practices in Judah (see 2 Kgs 23).

—*Jaime L. Waters*

Saul continues his attempts to get rid of David. Possibly on the wedding night itself, Saul's soldiers surround David's house in order to kill him in the morning. But Michal protects David. She helps him escape through a window and then puts the household idol, apparently a sizeable statue, into the bed so that the guards will suppose it is David. When the trick is discovered, Saul accuses Michal of preferring David to him, her father. She makes the excuse that David threatened her. It is evident that her love for David is primary in her life. Her love for David protects him from her father Saul.

One of David's Wives

2 Samuel 3:12-16

[12]Then Abner sent messengers to David in Telam, where he was at the moment, to say, "Make a covenant with me, and you have me on your side, to bring all Israel over to you." [13]He replied, "Good, I will make a covenant with you. But one thing I require of you. You must not appear before me unless you bring back Michal, Saul's daughter, when you come to present yourself to me." [14]At the same time David sent messengers to Ishbaal, son of Saul, to say, "Give me my wife Michal, whom I betrothed by paying a hundred Philistine foreskins." [15]Ishbaal sent for her and took her away from her husband Paltiel, son of Laish, [16]who followed her weeping as far as Bahurim. But Abner said to him, "Go back!" So he turned back.

When David fled from Saul (1 Sam 21:1), he did not take Michal with him. Subsequently he married Abigail, Ahinoam (1 Sam 25:39-43), Maacah, Haggith, Shephatiah, and Eglah (2 Sam 3:2-5). "But Saul gave David's wife Michal, Saul's own daughter, to Palti, son of Laish, who was from Gallim" (1 Sam 25:44).

After the death of Saul, David rules over Judah, and Saul's son Ishbaal rules over Israel, which consists of the other tribes (2 Sam 2:1-11). Ishbaal's power resides in his army general Abner. Abner, however, quarrels with Ishbaal over one of Saul's concubines, so Abner decides to switch allegiances to David (2 Sam 3:6-11). David agrees to welcome Abner but insists that the price of his acceptance is the return of Michal to him as a wife. So Michal is taken away from Paltiel, who follows her for some distance weeping, and she is added to David's growing harem.

Michal is again the pawn of men in power. In getting her back, David gains the possibility of uniting his dynasty with the house of Saul, thus gaining a double claim to rule over the twelve tribes. David and his descendants have a claim because of David's anointing as king (1 Sam 16); Saul's descendants (through Michal) have a claim because of the anointing of Saul (1 Sam 10). David also demonstrates his strength; Ishbaal is forced to send his sister to his rival king. No consideration is taken of the feelings of Michal, who seems to have been greatly loved by her second husband. Who can guess how she feels as she returns to be one of David's many wives?

Saul presents Michal to David

2 Samuel 6:16-23

[16]As the ark of the LORD was entering the City of David, Michal, daughter of Saul, looked down from her window, and when she saw King David jumping and dancing before the LORD, she despised him in her heart. [17]They brought in the ark of the LORD and set it in its place within the tent which David had pitched for it. Then David sacrificed burnt offerings and communion offerings before the LORD. [18]When David had finished sacrificing burnt offerings and communion offerings, he blessed the people in the name of the LORD of hosts, [19]and distributed among all the people, the entire multitude of Israel, to every man and every woman, one loaf of bread, one piece of meat, and one raisin cake. Then all the people returned to their homes.

[20]When David went home to bless his own house, Michal, the daughter of Saul, came out to meet him and said, "How well the king of Israel has honored himself today, exposing himself to the view of the slave girls of his followers, as a commoner might expose himself!" [21]But David replied to Michal: "I was dancing before the LORD. As the LORD lives, who chose me over your father and all his house when he appointed me ruler over the LORD's people, Israel, not only will I make merry before the LORD, [22]but I will demean myself even more. I will be lowly in your eyes, but in the eyes of the slave girls you spoke of I will be somebody." [23]Saul's daughter Michal was childless to the day she died.

The crisis described here comes as David reaches the peak of his power. He has conquered Jerusalem and made it his capital. Now he brings the ark of the covenant, a sign of God's presence, to his city so that Jerusalem might become the city of God. As David dances in celebration, Michal watches. She accosts him when he returns to the palace, scorning his public demonstration. In a scathing retort he reminds her that God has preferred the house

 David established a **harem of wives** whose names and son's names are recorded in Scripture:

	Wife of David	Son
1 Sam 18:27	Michal, Saul's daughter	No children (2 Sam 6:23)
1 Sam 25:40	Abigail, widow of Nabal	Chileab
1 Sam 25:43	Ahinoam of Jezreel	Amnon
2 Sam 3:3	Maacah, daughter of Talmai, king of Geshur	Absalom
2 Sam 3:4	Haggith	Adonijah
2 Sam 3:4	Abital	Shephatiah
2 Sam 3:5	Eglah	Ithream
2 Sam 11:27	Bathsheba, wife of Uriah	Solomon (2 Sam 12:24)

David had additional sons whose mothers are not named (2 Sam 5:13-16). The only daughter mentioned is Tamar, who is never acknowledged as David's daughter but only as Absalom's sister (2 Sam 13:1).

of David to the house of her father Saul. Whatever love that may have remained between these two members of rival royal families is now gone, as is the dream of uniting the two dynasties. Michal is doomed to seclusion in the harem for the rest of her life. David will never send for her. "Saul's daughter Michal was childless to the day she died."

Michal's story is a tragedy. The man she loved and whose life she saved uses her only as a claim to power. In the struggle she is taken from a man who loved her. She is a sacrifice to the claims of Israel's monarchy.

BATHSHEBA

Wife of Uriah

2 Samuel 11:1-5

[1]At the turn of the year, the time when kings go to war, David sent out Joab along with his officers and all Israel, and they laid waste the Ammonites and besieged Rabbah. David himself remained in Jerusalem. [2]One evening David rose from his bed and strolled about on the roof of the king's house. From the roof he saw a woman bathing; she was very beautiful. [3]David sent people to inquire about the woman and was told, "She is Bathsheba, daughter of Eliam, and wife of Uriah the Hittite, Joab's armor-bearer." [4]Then David sent messengers and took her. When she came to him, he took her to bed, at a time when she was just purified after her period; and she returned to her house. [5]But the woman had become pregnant; she sent a message to inform David, "I am pregnant."

Bathsheba is a beautiful woman, the wife of one of David's soldiers. When David sees her from his roof, he desires her. He sends for her, takes her sexually, and sends her home. There is no word of love or affection, but only lust, power, and self-gratification. When Bathsheba realizes that she has conceived, she speaks the

only words recorded of her in 2 Samuel: "I am pregnant." David's actions demonstrate an abuse of power. Bathsheba, as a woman and a foreigner, would have little choice when the messengers of the king came for her.

2 Samuel 11:6-17

[6]So David sent a message to Joab, "Send me Uriah the Hittite." Joab sent Uriah to David. [7]And when he came, David asked him how Joab was, how the army was, and how the war was going, and Uriah answered that all was well. [8]David then said to Uriah, "Go down to your house and bathe your feet." Uriah left the king's house, and a portion from the king's table was sent after him. [9]But Uriah slept at the entrance of the king's house with the other officers of his lord, and did not go down to his own house. [10]David was told, "Uriah has not gone down to his house." So he said to Uriah, "Have you not come from a journey? Why, then, did you not go down to your house?" [11]Uriah answered David, "The ark and Israel and Judah are staying in tents, and my lord Joab and my lord's servants are encamped in the open field. Can I go home to eat and to drink and to sleep with my wife? As the LORD lives and as you live, I will do no such thing." [12]Then David said to Uriah, "Stay here today also, and tomorrow I will send you back." So Uriah stayed in Jerusalem that day. On the following day, [13]David summoned him, and he ate and drank with David, who got him drunk. But in the evening he went out to sleep on his bed among his lord's servants, and did not go down to his house. [14]The next morning David wrote a letter to Joab which he sent by Uriah. [15]This is what he wrote in the letter: "Place Uriah up front, where the fighting is fierce. Then pull back and leave him to be struck down dead." [16]So while Joab was besieging the city, he assigned Uriah to a place where he knew the defenders were strong. [17]When the men of the city made a sortie against Joab, some officers of David's army fell, and Uriah the Hittite also died.

When David learns that Bathsheba is pregnant, he uses all his resources to cover up his action. First he sends for her husband, in the hope that Uriah will sleep with his wife. But Uriah, out of respect for the other soldiers in the field, will not go home. The second night David gets him drunk, hoping that he will go to Bathsheba, but again Uriah spends the night in the barracks. So David determines that Uriah must die. Uriah carries his own death warrant to the commander, an order from David that Uriah be abandoned at the front lines. Bathsheba's husband is to be killed in order to protect the king. David shows no concern for Bathsheba herself. Her loss will be grave. Her husband Uriah is a noble soldier, single-hearted in his devotion to duty and loyalty to the king. David, father of the child she carries, is intent only on covering his guilt, even to the point of murder.

2 Samuel 11:18-25

[18]Then Joab sent David a report of all the details of the battle, [19]instructing the messenger, "When you have finished giving the king all the details of the battle, [20]the king may become angry and say to you: 'Why did you go near the city to fight? Did you not know that they would shoot from the wall above? [21]Who killed Abimelech, son of Jerubbaal? Was it not a woman who threw a millstone down on him from the wall above, so that he died in Thebez? Why did you go near the wall?' Then you in turn are to say, 'Your servant Uriah the Hittite is also dead.'" [22]The messenger set out, and on his arrival he reported to David everything Joab had sent him to tell. [23]He told David: "The men had the advantage over us and came out into the open against us, but we pushed them back to the entrance of the city gate. [24]Then the archers shot at your servants from the wall above, and some of the king's servants died; and your servant Uriah the Hittite is also dead."

[25]David said to the messenger: "This is what you shall say to Joab: 'Do not let this be a great evil in your sight, for the sword devours now here and now there. Strengthen your attack on the city and destroy it.' Encourage him."

Joab carries out David's orders and sends a message to the king that Uriah is dead. Included in the message is a reference to Abimilech, the king of Shechem who was killed when a woman threw a millstone down on his head. The obvious connection is to the questionable strategy of placing troops too close to the city wall. Joab may also be expressing his opinion that, just as a woman killed Abimilech, a woman (Bathsheba) killed Uriah. Or perhaps Joab is suggesting that this incident will be as deadly for David, the king, as the incident at Thebez was deadly for another king, Abimilech.

Wife of David

2 Samuel 11:26-27

[26]When the wife of Uriah heard that her husband had died, she mourned her lord. [27]But once the mourning was over, David sent for her and brought her into his house. She became his wife and bore him a son. But in the sight of the LORD what David had done was evil.

Bathsheba mourns for her dead husband and then is brought to the palace to join the other wives of David. There is no indication as to whether she goes willingly or not. There is also no description of the depth of her grief. Her choice and preference are not mentioned throughout the story. In due time the child of the king is born to her.

"But in the sight of the LORD what David had done was evil." David has committed adultery, arranged for the husband's murder, and taken the widow as his wife.

---

2 Samuel 12:1-12

¹The LORD sent Nathan to David, and when he came to him, he said: "Tell me how you judge this case: In a certain town there were two men, one rich, the other poor. ²The rich man had flocks and herds in great numbers. ³But the poor man had nothing at all except one little ewe lamb that he had bought. He nourished her, and she grew up with him and his children. Of what little he had she ate; from his own cup she drank; in his bosom she slept; she was like a daughter to him. ⁴Now, a visitor came to the rich man, but he spared his own flocks and herds to prepare a meal for the traveler who had come to him: he took the poor man's ewe lamb and prepared it for the one who had come to him." ⁵David grew very angry with that man and said to Nathan: "As the LORD lives, the man who has done this deserves death! ⁶He shall make fourfold restitution for the lamb because he has done this and was unsparing." ⁷Then Nathan said to David: "You are the man!

"Thus says the LORD God of Israel: I anointed you king over Israel. I delivered you from the hand of Saul. ⁸I gave you your lord's house and your lord's wives for your own. I gave you the house of Israel and of Judah. And if this were not enough, I could count up for you still more. ⁹Why have you despised the LORD and done what is evil in his sight? You have cut down Uriah the Hittite with the sword; his wife you took as your own, and him you killed with the sword of the Ammonites. ¹⁰Now, therefore, the sword shall never depart from your house, because you have despised me and have taken the wife of Uriah the Hittite to be your wife. ¹¹Thus says the LORD: I will bring evil upon you out of your own house. I will take your wives before your very eyes, and will give them to your neighbor: he shall lie with your wives in broad daylight. ¹²You have acted in secret, but I will do this in the presence of all Israel, in the presence of the sun itself."

The Hebrew word **mashal** connotes a wise saying, often in the form of **a short proverb or a parable**. The root meaning of *mashal* means either "to rule" or "to compare." Proverbs and parables often use comparisons, for example, "The kingdom of heaven is like . . ." (see Matt 13:31, 33, etc.). Good proverbs and parables also "rule" in that they lead us to see things differently, to change our minds, even to judge ourselves. Nathan's story is a good example of a *mashal* (2 Sam 12:1-4). David's actions are compared to those of a selfish rich man; the story leads David to pronounce judgment against himself.

David's court prophet Nathan uses a parable to lead the king to pass judgment on himself: "[T]he man who has done this deserves death!" Nathan's parable convicts David as the guilty party, the one who took another man's wife. Bathsheba is portrayed as a little ewe lamb, helpless as she is stolen from one man to feed the appetite of another. The parable indicates that in the encounter she has died. Certainly her life has been irrevocably changed.

David's sin will lead to suffering for his other wives and for many innocent members of his family throughout future generations. His child will die (2 Sam 12:18). His daughter Tamar will be raped and cast aside (2 Sam 13:1-22). His sons will be killed (2 Sam 13:28-29; 18:14-15). His wives will be shamed and handed over to others (2 Sam 16:21-22).

---

2 Samuel 12:13-25

¹³Then David said to Nathan, "I have sinned against the LORD." Nathan answered David: "For his part, the LORD has removed your sin. You shall not die, ¹⁴but since you have utterly spurned the LORD by this deed, the child born to you will surely die." ¹⁵Then Nathan returned to his house.

The LORD struck the child that the wife of Uriah had borne to David, and it became desperately ill. [16]David pleaded with God on behalf of the child. He kept a total fast, and spent the night lying on the ground clothed in sackcloth. [17]The elders of his house stood beside him to get him to rise from the ground; but he would not, nor would he take food with them. [18]On the seventh day, the child died. David's servants were afraid to tell him that the child was dead, for they said: "When the child was alive, we spoke to him, but he would not listen to what we said. How can we tell him the child is dead? He may do some harm!" [19]But David noticed his servants whispering among themselves and realized that the child was dead. He asked his servants, "Is the child dead?" They said, "Yes." [20]Rising from the ground, David washed and anointed himself, and changed his clothes. Then he went to the house of the LORD and worshiped. He returned to his own house and asked for food; they set it before him, and he ate. [21]His servants said to him: "What is this you are doing? While the child was living, you fasted and wept and kept vigil; now that the child is dead, you rise and take food." [22]He replied: "While the child was living, I fasted and wept, thinking, 'Who knows? The LORD may grant me the child's life.' [23]But now he is dead. Why should I fast? Can I bring him back again? I shall go to him, but he will not return to me." [24]Then David consoled Bathsheba his wife. He went and slept with her; and she conceived and bore him a son, who was named Solomon. The LORD loved him [25]and sent the prophet Nathan to name him Jedidiah, on behalf of the LORD.

David repents of his sins of adultery and murder. The guilt may be David's, but the punishment falls on Bathsheba as well: her son will die. The royal house to which she has come will be filled with violence. The narrator describes David's grief; Bathsheba's grief is only hinted at in the mention of David's comfort. (This is the only time that David expresses concern for Bathsheba's feelings.) She conceives a second son by this man who has brought her so much

sorrow. This second son, Solomon, is beloved by the Lord, a gift of God's grace.

Bathsheba's future is now dependent on the fate of her son. She disappears from the story until he grows to manhood.

Mother of Solomon

1 Kings 1:11-34

[11]Then Nathan said to Bathsheba, Solomon's mother: "Have you not heard that Adonijah, son of Haggith, has become king, and our lord David does not know? [12]Come now, let me advise you so that you may save your life and the life of your son Solomon. [13]Go, visit King David, and say to him, 'Did you not, my lord king, swear to your handmaid: Your son Solomon shall be king after me; it is he who shall sit upon my throne? Why, then, has Adonijah become king?' [14]And while you are still there speaking to the king, I will come in after you and confirm your words."

[15]So Bathsheba visited the king in his room. The king was very old, and Abishag the Shunamite was caring for the king. [16]Bathsheba bowed in homage to the king. The king said to her, "What do you wish?" [17]She answered him: "My lord, you swore to your servant by the LORD, your God, 'Solomon your son will be king after me; it is he who shall sit upon my throne.' [18]But now Adonijah has become king, and you, my lord king, do not know it. [19]He has sacrificed bulls, fatlings, and sheep in great numbers; he has invited all the king's sons, Abiathar the priest, and Joab, the commander of the army, but not your servant Solomon. [20]Now, my lord king, all Israel is looking to you to declare to them who is to sit upon the throne of my lord the king after him. [21]If this is not done, when my lord the king rests with his ancestors, I and my son Solomon will be considered criminals."

[22]While she was still speaking to the king, Nathan the prophet came in. [23]They told the king,

continue

"Nathan the prophet is here." He entered the king's presence and did him homage, bowing to the floor. ²⁴Then Nathan said: "My lord king, did you say, 'Adonijah shall be king after me and shall sit upon my throne'? ²⁵For today he went down and sacrificed bulls, fatlings, and sheep in great numbers; he invited all the king's sons, the commanders of the army, and Abiathar the priest, and even now they are eating and drinking in his company and saying, 'Long live King Adonijah!' ²⁶But me, your servant, he did not invite; nor Zadok the priest, nor Benaiah, son of Jehoiada, nor your servant Solomon. ²⁷If this was done by order of my lord the king, you did not tell me, your servant, who is to sit upon the throne of my lord the king after him."

²⁸King David answered, "Call Bathsheba here." When she entered the king's presence and stood before him, ²⁹the king swore, "As the LORD lives, who has redeemed my life from all distress, ³⁰this very day I will fulfill the oath I swore to you by the LORD, the God of Israel, 'Your son Solomon shall be king after me and shall sit upon my throne in my place.'" ³¹Bowing to the floor in homage to the king, Bathsheba said, "May my lord, King David, live forever!"

³²Then King David said, "Call Zadok the priest, Nathan the prophet, and Benaiah, son of Jehoiada." When they had entered the king's presence, ³³he said to them: "Take with you the royal officials. Mount my son Solomon upon my own mule and escort him down to Gihon. ³⁴There Zadok the priest and Nathan the prophet shall anoint him king over Israel, and you shall blow the ram's horn and cry, 'Long live King Solomon!'

Bathsheba reappears at the critical moment when the successor to David must be decided. Two of David's sons have been eliminated from the choice: Amnon and Absalom are dead. Adonijah is now planning to be the next king. The crisis brings Bathsheba and Nathan together again. Nathan concocts a plot. First Bathsheba will suggest to the elderly king that he had promised that her son Solomon would succeed him on the throne. Then Nathan will come in and remind the king of the same promise. It is unclear whether David actually made this promise·or not. It is possible that the promise is simply Nathan's invention.

David and Bathsheba's child dies. Julius Schnorr von Carolsfeld (1860)

The scheming of Nathan and Bathsheba is successful. David orders the anointing of Solomon as king. In proposing the plot Nathan says to Bathsheba, "Come now, let me advise you so that you may save your life and the life of your son Solomon." His suggestion is a reminder that the lives of rival heirs to the throne and the lives of their mothers are in danger. Nathan appeals to Bathsheba's fear and sense of survival. Once more Bathsheba's future is dependent on the will of the king and the fate of her son.

In this scene Bathsheba shows herself to be a woman of power in contrast to two other women, Abishag and Haggith. Abishag is present when Bathsheba enters. She is a passive character throughout the story, having been brought to the king to attend him, to nurse him, and to keep him warm. But she is not a sexual partner of the king (1 Kgs 1:2-4); she is not the mother of any of his sons. She never speaks; she exercises no power. Haggith is the mother of David's son, Adonijah. She too is wronged by David. She loses her son in the struggle for the throne (1 Kgs 2:23-25). We do not know what becomes of her. It is the son of Bathsheba, the one whom "the LORD loved" (2 Sam 12:24), who succeeds his father David.

---

1 Kings 2:12-25

[12]Then Solomon sat on the throne of David his father, and his kingship was established.
[13]Adonijah, son of Haggith, came to Bathsheba, the mother of Solomon. "Do you come in peace?" she asked. "In peace," he answered, [14]and he added, "I have something to say to you." She replied, "Speak." [15]So he said: "You know that the kingship was mine, and all Israel expected me to be king. But the kingship passed me by and went to my brother; by the LORD's will it went to him. [16]But now there is one favor I would ask of you. Do not refuse me." And she said, "Speak on." [17]He said, "Please ask King Solomon, who will not refuse you, to give me Abishag the Shunamite to be my wife." [18]Bathsheba replied, "Very well, I will speak to the king for you."

[19]Then Bathsheba went to King Solomon to speak to him for Adonijah, and the king stood up to meet her and paid her homage. Then he sat down upon his throne, and a throne was provided for the king's mother, who sat at his right. [20]She said, "There is one small favor I would ask of you. Do not refuse me." The king said to her, "Ask it, my mother, for I will not refuse you." [21]So she said, "Let Abishag the Shunamite be given to your brother Adonijah to be his wife." [22]King Solomon answered his mother, "And why do you ask that Abishag the Shunamite be given to Adonijah? Ask the kingship for him as well, for he is my older brother! Ask for him, for Abiathar the priest, for Joab, son of Zeruiah!" [23]And King Solomon swore by the LORD: "May God do thus to me and more, if Adonijah has not spoken this word at the cost of his life. [24]And now, as the LORD lives, who has established me and set me on the throne of David my father and made for me a house as he promised, this day shall Adonijah be put to death." [25]Then King Solomon sent Benaiah, son of Jehoiada, who struck him dead.

The fate of rivals for the throne is demonstrated in the story of Adonijah. He comes to enlist Bathsheba's aid in acquiring David's last concubine. She does as Adonijah asks. The request is not as simple as it seems, however. Possession of the king's concubines demonstrates the power of the throne. When Absalom revolted against David, his taking of the king's concubines in public view was a claim to the king's power (2 Sam 16:21-22). Solomon sees the request for Abishag as a threat and orders the death of Adonijah.

Once more Bathsheba's motives are not revealed. Does she ask in innocence as a favor to Adonijah? Or is her action a subtle way of removing a threat to her son's rule and her own security? The narrator leaves us to wonder.

Bathsheba's position in Solomon's court is noteworthy. She is the first biblical "queen mother," a position of political and religious power and influence. Fifteen of the subsequent passages listing the succession of a king to the throne also name his mother (1 Kgs 15:2; 22:42; 2 Kgs 8:26; 12:2; 14:2; 15:2, 33; 18:2; 21:1, 19; 22:1; 23:31, 36; 24:8, 18).[1] (See Endnotes on p. 102.)

Memory of Bathsheba

Bathsheba is mentioned only three more times in the Bible. In 1 Chronicles she is named as the mother of four of David's sons (3:5), but the story of David's adultery and murder of her husband is omitted by the Chronicler. The title of Psalm 51 indicates that the psalm is a "psalm of David, when Nathan the prophet came to him after he had gone in to Bathsheba" (vv. 1-2). Bathsheba is also one of the five women mentioned in Matthew's genealogy of Jesus, though her name is not used: "David became the father of Solomon, whose mother had been the wife of Uriah" (1:6).

The story of Bathsheba is complicated and incomplete. Her first husband is killed by her second. Her first son dies as a punishment to the king; her second son succeeds him. She is of major significance in God's fulfillment of the promise to David that one of his sons will sit upon his throne (2 Sam 7). Solomon is associated with a variety of accomplishments, such as building the temple, acquiring wealth and a reputation for wisdom, and ruling over a united kingdom. But Bathsheba's own motivations, intentions, and desires are never revealed. She is seen only through the stories of the powerful men who surround her.

TAMAR

A Sister Desired

2 Samuel 13:1-6

[1]After this, the following occurred. David's son Absalom had a beautiful sister named Tamar, and David's son Amnon loved her. [2]He was in such anguish over his sister Tamar that he became sick; she was a virgin, and Amnon thought it impossible to do anything to her. [3]Now Amnon had a friend named Jonadab, son of David's brother Shimeah, who was very clever. [4]He asked him, "Prince, why are you so dejected morning after morning? Why not tell me?" So Amnon said to him, "I am in love with Tamar, my brother Absalom's sister." [5]Then Jonadab replied, "Lie down on your bed and pretend to be sick. When your father comes to visit you, say to him, 'Please let my sister Tamar come and encourage me to take food. If she prepares something in my presence, for me to see, I will eat it from her hand.'" [6]So Amnon lay down and pretended to be sick. When the king came to visit him, Amnon said to the king, "Please let my sister Tamar come and prepare some fried cakes before my eyes, that I may take food from her hand."

In the story of Tamar, the structure of the first sentence illustrates her situation. She is a sister caught between two brothers. The two brothers are each named "David's son," but Tamar is never identified as "David's daugh-

Detail from Absalom and Tamar *by Guercino (1591-1666)*

ter," though she is his daughter. Each brother has his own claim on her; after the disaster her father never claims her.

We also learn in the first paragraph that Tamar is beautiful and that she is a virgin. These qualities will lead to her destruction. Her half-brother Amnon is so infatuated with her beauty that he makes himself sick. Since she is a virgin and thus valuable to the king as a possible wife for a foreign prince, Amnon knows he cannot have her. But his friends encourage him to set up a situation in which he can be alone with Tamar. Then he can do to her whatever he wishes.

---

2 Samuel 13:7-13

[7]David then sent home a message to Tamar, "Please go to the house of your brother Amnon and prepare some food for him." [8]Tamar went to the house of her brother Amnon, who was in bed. Taking dough and kneading it, she twisted it into cakes before his eyes and fried the cakes. [9]Then she took the pan and set out the cakes before him. But Amnon would not eat; he said, "Have everyone leave me." When they had all left him, [10]Amnon said to Tamar, "Bring the food into the bedroom, that I may have it from your hand." So Tamar picked up the cakes she had prepared and brought them to her brother Amnon in the bedroom. [11]But when she brought them close to him so he could eat, he seized her and said to her, "Come! Lie with me, my sister!" [12]But she answered him, "No, my brother! Do not force me! This is not done in Israel. Do not commit this terrible crime. [13]Where would I take my shame? And you would be labeled a fool in Israel. So please, speak to the king; he will not keep me from you."

David falls for the plot and sends Tamar to Amnon. She prepares the food and presents it to him, but he will not eat. He insists on being fed—alone—at her hand. When everyone else has left, he attempts first to seduce her. Like his father, Amnon seeks sexual intimacy with a woman without regard for her desires. Tamar

makes a counter-offer, suggesting that the king might give her to Amnon as a wife. She clearly has a strong sense of her own honor and self-preservation. She is willing to find a solution that will protect her and satisfy Amnon's lust.

A Sister Raped and Rejected

---

2 Samuel 13:14-22

[14]But he would not listen to her; he was too strong for her: he forced her down and raped her. [15]Then Amnon felt intense hatred for her; the hatred he felt for her far surpassed the love he had had for her. Amnon said to her, "Get up, leave." [16]She replied, "No, brother, because sending me away would be far worse than this evil thing you have done to me." He would not listen to her, [17]but called the youth who was his attendant and said, "Send this girl outside, away from me, and bar the door after her." [18]Now she had on a long tunic, for that is how virgin princesses dressed in olden days. When his attendant put her out and barred the door after her, [19]Tamar put ashes on her head and tore the long tunic in which she was clothed. Then, putting her hands to her head, she went away crying loudly. [20]Her brother Absalom said to her: "Has your brother Amnon been with you? Keep still now, my sister; he is your brother. Do not take this so to heart." So Tamar remained, devastated, in the house of her brother Absalom. [21]King David, when he heard of the whole affair, became very angry. He would not, however, antagonize Amnon, his high-spirited son; he loved him, because he was his first-born. [22]And Absalom said nothing, good or bad, to Amnon; but Absalom hated Amnon for having humiliated his sister Tamar.

Amnon refuses to listen to Tamar. He rapes her, and then he hates her. In spite of her pleas, he throws her out of the house and locks the door. Weeping, she tears the garment that signifies her virginal status. She goes to her full brother Absalom, who conceives a terrible hatred for Amnon. David, however, does nothing because he does not want to offend his first-born son.

The occurrences of the family words "brother," "sister," and "son" reveal the irony of Tamar's tragedy. Although Tamar's "family" relationship to Amnon and to David is repeatedly mentioned, the relationship is distorted and ignored by both men. The *sister* is caught between the two *sons* (13:1). Amnon is in distress over his *sister* (13:2) and tells his friend that he is in love with his *brother's sister* (13:4). His friend advises him to ask his *father* to send his *sister* (13:5). So Amnon asks the king to send his *sister*, and David sends her to her *brother* (13:6-7). Tamar goes to the house of her *brother* (13:8), bakes cakes, and brings them to her *brother* (13:10). He says, "Lie with me, my *sister*" (13:11), but she refuses, "No, my *brother*" (13:12). After he has raped her and wants to drive her out, she protests, "No, *brother*" (13:16). She flees to her *brother* Absalom who says, "Has your *brother* Amnon been with you? Keep still now, my *sister*; he is your *brother*." But she remains devastated "in the house of her *brother*" (13:20). David does not want to offend his *son* (13:21), but Absalom hates Amnon for raping his *sister* (13:22). The word "sister" occurs eight times in this passage, "brother" ten times, "son" three times, and "father" once.

Memory of Tamar

In spite of the abundance of references to family relationships, Tamar is never called David's daughter. The word "daughter" does not even occur in the passage. Its next appearance is in a reference to Absalom's children: "Absalom had three sons born to him, besides a daughter named Tamar, who was a beautiful woman" (14:27). This daughter is undoubtedly named for Absalom's sister, perhaps in grief, perhaps as a way to honor Tamar.

Tamar's tragedy is part of David's punishment for his adultery with Bathsheba and the murder of her husband. It is part of the violence that Nathan predicted would never depart from the house of David (12:10). The tragedy also has a direct effect on the succession to David's throne. Amnon was the supposed heir, but in revenge for his rape of Tamar, Absalom murders him (13:23-33). Then Absalom, another possible heir, flees (13:34-38). Even when he returns, he is never fully reconciled to the king (14:28-33). Eventually he mounts a revolt and drives David from Jerusalem (15:1-18). The revolt is put down, and Absalom is killed (18:1-18), thus removing another heir to the throne. Throughout the story David grieves over his sons (12:16; 13:39; 19:1-5). There is never a word of grief over his daughter.

QUEEN OF SHEBA

1 Kings 10:1-13

[1]The queen of Sheba, having heard a report of Solomon's fame, came to test him with subtle questions. [2]She arrived in Jerusalem with a very numerous retinue, and with camels bearing spices, a large amount of gold, and precious stones. She came to Solomon and spoke to him about everything that she had on her mind. [3]King Solomon explained everything she asked about, and there was nothing so obscure that the king could not explain it to her. [4]When the queen of Sheba witnessed Solomon's great wisdom, the house he had built, [5]the food at his table, the seating of his ministers, the attendance and dress of his waiters, his servers, and the burnt offerings he offered in the house of the LORD, it took her breath away. [6]"The report I heard in my country about your deeds and your wisdom is true," she told the king. [7]"I did not believe the report until I came and saw with my own eyes that not even the half had been told me. Your wisdom and prosperity surpass the report I heard. [8]Happy are your servants, happy these ministers of yours, who stand before

you always and listen to your wisdom. ⁹Blessed be the LORD, your God, who has been pleased to place you on the throne of Israel. In his enduring love for Israel, the LORD has made you king to carry out judgment and justice." ¹⁰Then she gave the king one hundred and twenty gold talents, a very large quantity of spices, and precious stones. Never again did anyone bring such an abundance of spices as the queen of Sheba gave to King Solomon.

¹¹Hiram's fleet, which used to bring gold from Ophir, also brought from there a very large quantity of almug wood and precious stones. ¹²With this wood the king made supports for the house of the LORD and for the house of the king, and harps and lyres for the singers. Never again was any such almug wood brought or seen to the present day.

¹³King Solomon gave the queen of Sheba everything she desired and asked for, besides what King Solomon gave her from Solomon's royal bounty. Then she returned with her servants to her own country.

Sheba (or Seba) is probably a tribe of northwestern Arabia. Sheba is listed as a caravan people by Job (Job 6:19), and the Sabeans carry off Job's farm animals in the prologue to his book (Job 1:15; cf. Joel 4:8). They are traders of incense (Jer 6:20), precious stones, gold, and textiles (Ezek 27:22-24). The wealth of Seba/Sheba is indicated in several places (Ps 72:10; cf. Isa 60:6).

Even though Sheba is generally agreed to be an Arabian tribe, there is a contrasting tradition that locates Sheba with the Ethiopians. Genesis 10:7 lists Seba as one of the descendants of Cush (Ethiopia). Josephus, a first-century Jewish historian, also assumes the queen comes from Ethiopia. There is a tradition in Ethiopia that the kings are descended from Solomon and the queen of Sheba. This royal line, called the "House of Solomon," remained in power in Ethiopia until 1974.

According to the biblical story the queen of Sheba comes to Solomon to test his wisdom. In fact, she probably came to him to confirm trad-

ing agreements since trade was an important part of the Solomonic program (1 Kgs 9:26-28; 10:14-29). The queen arrives with "camels bearing spices, a large amount of gold, and precious stones" (10:2). Before she leaves, she gives the king a great abundance of treasures (10:10). Solomon also gives her presents (10:13). The trading agreement seems to have been sealed.

Wisdom, however, is also an important part of Solomon's character. "He was wiser than anyone else . . . and his fame spread throughout the neighboring peoples. . . . People from all nations came to hear Solomon's wisdom, sent by all the kings of the earth who had heard of his wisdom" (1 Kgs 5:11, 14). The queen is also wise; she has come to test Solomon with subtle questions (10:1). But Solomon is greater than she imagined; she is overwhelmed by his wisdom. She recognizes that Solomon's wisdom is a gift of God, a sign of God's love for Israel (10:9). She is impressed by Solomon's wealth and the culture of his court, added signs of his wisdom.

The queen of Sheba is an important witness to the wealth and wisdom of Solomon. She also gives praise to the Lord, Israel's God. Jesus recalls her openness to learning from Solomon, contrasting it with the hardness of heart of his own contemporaries: "At the judgment the queen of the south will arise with this generation and condemn it, because she came from the ends of the earth to hear the wisdom of Solomon; and there is something greater than Solomon here" (Matt 12:42; cf. Luke 11:31).

JEZEBEL
Queen of Israel

1 Kings 16:29-33

²⁹Ahab, son of Omri, became king of Israel in the thirty-eighth year of Asa, king of Judah. Ahab, son of Omri, reigned over Israel in Samaria for twenty-two years.

continue

³⁰Ahab, son of Omri, did what was evil in the LORD's sight more than any of his predecessors. ³¹It was not enough for him to follow the sins of Jeroboam, son of Nebat. He even married Jezebel, daughter of Ethbaal, king of the Sidonians, and began to serve Baal, and worship him. ³²Ahab set up an altar to Baal in the house of Baal which he built in Samaria, ³³and also made an asherah. Ahab did more to provoke the LORD, the God of Israel, to anger than any of the kings of Israel before him.

Rival of Elijah

1 Kings 18:2-4

Now the famine in Samaria was severe, ³and Ahab had summoned Obadiah, master of his palace, who greatly revered the LORD. ⁴When Jezebel was slaughtering the prophets of the LORD, Obadiah took a hundred prophets, hid them away by fifties in caves, and supplied them with food and water.

1 Kings 19:1-3

¹Ahab told Jezebel all that Elijah had done—that he had murdered all the prophets by the sword. ²Jezebel then sent a messenger to Elijah and said, "May the gods do thus to me and more, if by this time tomorrow I have not done with your life what was done to each of them." ³Elijah was afraid and fled for his life, going to Beer-sheba of Judah.

Jezebel is the daughter of Ethbaal, the king of the Phoenicians, who are also called Sidonians, as one of their primary cities was Sidon. Jezebel becomes the wife of Ahab, king of Israel. Ahab belongs to the dynasty of Omri, one of the most prosperous of Israel's dynasties. Other peoples of the ancient Near East continued to call Israel "the house of Omri" long after the dynasty had disappeared.

Phoenicia was located on the Mediterranean coast north of Israel. Two of its major cities were Tyre and Sidon. These Phoenician ports prospered through the production of purple goods and the shipping trade. The Phoenicians, like the Canaanites, worshiped the god Baal. When Jezebel came to Israel she brought with her prophets of Baal and encouraged worship of him. Ahab, like Solomon before him, built a shrine for the worship of his wife's god (see 1 Kgs 11:4-10).

The biblical stories of the kings of Israel (the northern kingdom) are told by writers from Judah (the southern kingdom). The books of Samuel include traditions that remember or envision a united kingdom under David. After the death of his son Solomon, the kingdom split into two kingdoms, Israel and Judah. Almost a century later, Jezebel and Ahab ruled in the northern kingdom of Israel. Much of the books of Kings portrays northern royals in a negative light, as told by authors in the southern kingdom.

Jezebel and the prophet Elijah become mortal enemies. Each sees the other's unflinching devotion to a particular god as a deadly threat. Jezebel murders the prophets of Yahweh; Elijah, in a mocking contest, defeats and murders the prophets of Baal (1 Kgs 18). Jezebel, exercising her royal authority, condemns Elijah to death, and he flees.

The names of the two enemies express their bitter opposition. In the Septuagint (Greek) version of this text, Jezebel says to Elijah: "If you are Elijah, I am Jezebel" (19:2). The name "Elijah" means "Yahweh is my God." The name "Jezebel" probably means "The Prince [Baal] is mine." Jezebel and Elijah are a matched pair, each committed to his or her god.

Murder of Naboth

1 Kings 21:1-26

¹Naboth the Jezreelite had a vineyard in Jezreel next to the palace of Ahab, king of Samaria. Some time later, ²Ahab said to Naboth, "Give me your vineyard to be my vegetable garden, since it is close by, next to my house. I will give you a better vineyard in exchange, or, if you prefer, I will give you its value in money." ³Naboth said to Ahab, "The LORD forbid that I should give you my ancestral heritage." ⁴Ahab went home disturbed and angry at the answer Naboth the Jezreelite had given him: "I will not give you my ancestral heritage." Lying down on his bed, he turned away and would not eat. ⁵His wife Jezebel came to him and said to him, "Why are you so sullen that you will not eat?" ⁶He answered her, "Because I spoke to Naboth the Jezreelite and said to him, 'Sell me your vineyard, or, if you prefer, I will give you a vineyard in exchange.' But he said, 'I will not give you my vineyard.'" ⁷Jezebel his wife said to him, "What a king of Israel you are! Get up! Eat and be cheerful. I will give you the vineyard of Naboth the Jezreelite."

⁸So she wrote letters in Ahab's name and, having sealed them with his seal, sent them to the elders and to the nobles who lived in the same city with Naboth. ⁹This is what she wrote in the letters: "Proclaim a fast and set Naboth at the head of the people. ¹⁰Next, set two scoundrels opposite him to accuse him: 'You have cursed God and king.' Then take him out and stone him to death."

¹¹His fellow citizens—the elders and the nobles who dwelt in his city—did as Jezebel had ordered in the letters she sent them. ¹²They proclaimed a fast and set Naboth at the head of the people. ¹³Two scoundrels came in and sat opposite Naboth, and the scoundrels accused him in the presence of the people, "Naboth has cursed God and king." And they led him out of the city and stoned him to death. ¹⁴Then they sent word to Jezebel: "Naboth has been stoned to death."

¹⁵When Jezebel learned that Naboth had been stoned to death, she said to Ahab, "Go, take possession of the vineyard of Naboth the Jezreelite which he refused to sell you, because Naboth is not alive, but dead." ¹⁶When Ahab heard that Naboth was dead, he started on his way down to the vineyard of Naboth the Jezreelite, to take possession of it.

¹⁷Then the word of the LORD came to Elijah the Tishbite: ¹⁸Go down to meet Ahab, king of Israel, who is in Samaria. He will be in the vineyard of Naboth, where he has gone to take possession. ¹⁹Tell him: "Thus says the LORD: After murdering, do you also take possession?" And tell him, "Thus says the LORD: In the place where the dogs licked up the blood of Naboth, the dogs shall lick up your blood, too."

²⁰Ahab said to Elijah, "Have you found me out, my enemy?" He said, "I have found you. Because you have given yourself up to doing evil in the LORD's sight, ²¹I am bringing evil upon you: I will consume you and will cut off every male belonging to Ahab, whether bond or free, in Israel. ²²I will make your house like that of Jeroboam, son of Nebat, and like the house of Baasha, son of Ahijah, because you have provoked me by leading Israel into sin."

²³Against Jezebel, too, the LORD declared: The dogs shall devour Jezebel in the confines of Jezreel.

²⁴Anyone of Ahab's line who dies in the city,
    dogs will devour;
Anyone who dies in the field,
    the birds of the sky will devour.

²⁵Indeed, no one gave himself up to the doing of evil in the sight of the LORD as did Ahab, urged on by his wife Jezebel. ²⁶He became completely abominable by going after idols, just as the Amorites had done, whom the LORD drove out of the Israelites' way.

In the story of Naboth's vineyard, Jezebel appears ruthless. She does not understand the importance of land to the Israelite. She does not know the significance of land as a sign of participation in the covenant. Thus she cannot understand Naboth's insistence on keeping his vineyard. Why will he not sell or trade it? Neither does she understand the relationship between the king and the law in Israel. She does not see that the king, too, is subject to the law of Israel, which is the law of God. Thus she does not understand the hesitation of her husband. Why does he not simply exercise his royal power and seize the vineyard?

If Ahab will not act as king, she will act as queen. She takes matters into her own hands. As David had arranged the death of Uriah, Jezebel arranges the death of Naboth. According to Israelite law, a man could be condemned if the testimony of two witnesses agreed. Jezebel commands the people to produce two accusers, and Naboth is executed. Then Jezebel returns to her husband to announce that it is possible for him to take possession of the coveted vineyard.

On the way to the vineyard Ahab encounters Elijah, who announces the doom of the house of Ahab because of the murder of Naboth. The doom centers on Ahab; Jezebel is mentioned only parenthetically. Ahab will be punished because he listened to her; she, too, will die a horrible death. Because he responds to Elijah's announcement with humility and repentance, Ahab is spared (1 Kgs 21:27-29). Nothing more is said here of Jezebel's fate.

The kings of Israel expanded Israel's power and status in the region by marrying women with valuable political connections. Loyalty to particular gods made little difference in these marriages that were more like corporate mergers. It would take many centuries for a **theology of marriage** to develop that reflects the mutual love between two people who are both made in God's image.

Death of Jezebel

2 Kings 9:30-37

[30]Jehu came to Jezreel, and when Jezebel heard of it, she shadowed her eyes, adorned her hair, and looked down from her window. [31]As Jehu came through the gate, she cried out, "Is all well, you Zimri, murderer of your master?" [32]Jehu looked up to the window and shouted, "Who is on my side? Who?" At this, two or three eunuchs looked down toward him. [33]"Throw her down," he ordered. They threw her down, and some of her blood spurted against the wall and against the horses. Jehu trod over her body [34]and, after eating and drinking, he said: "Attend to that accursed woman and bury her; for she was the daughter of a king." [35]But when they went to bury her, they found nothing of her but the skull, the feet, and the hands. [36]They returned to Jehu, and when they told him, he said, "This is the word the LORD spoke through his servant Elijah the Tishbite: In the confines of Jezreel the dogs shall devour the flesh of Jezebel. [37]The corpse of Jezebel shall be like dung in the field in the confines of Jezreel, so that no one can say: This was Jezebel."

The death of Jezebel represents the final encounter between Jezebel and Elijah. When Elijah fled from Jezebel's anger, he went to Mount Horeb (Sinai). There God spoke to him in "a light silent sound" (1 Kgs 19:12). God commissioned Elijah to raise three people to power: Elisha as prophet after him, Hazael as king of Syria, Jehu as king of Israel. Elijah appoints Elisha who carries out the other two parts of the commission. When Elisha anoints Jehu as king, Jehu gathers an army and kills the kings of both Israel and Judah along with most of the royal families (2 Kgs 9). Among those killed are seventy of Ahab's descendants, thus fulfilling Elijah's prophecy against the house of Ahab (2 Kgs 10:1-11). Ahab himself is already dead.

Jehu also sets out against Jezebel. She dresses herself as befits a queen in order to meet her adversary. She addresses him as Zimri, who had assassinated Elah, king of Israel, a little more than thirty years before. Zimri himself ruled only seven days and killed himself during the attack by Omri, Jezebel's father-in-law (1 Kgs 16:9-15). Royal to the last, she scorns Jehu and predicts that his reign will be short, a prediction that did not come to pass.

Jezebel is thrown to the ground by her servants and dies. But when Jehu decides to give her a burial befitting a king's daughter, he is too late. As Elijah had prophesied, the dogs have eaten her flesh: "[N]o one can say: This was Jezebel."

Memory of Jezebel

Jezebel has become a symbol for the worst that can be said about women. Because she puts on her makeup and dresses in her royal finery to meet Jehu, she has been identified as a whore (see Rev 2:20). There is no indication in the text that this identification is true. When Jehu accuses her of fornication and witchcraft (9:22), it is probably a reference to her worship of Baal. She is also considered to be a power-hungry woman who will eliminate anyone who stands in her way. Her treatment of Naboth supports this idea. It must be remembered, however, that Jezebel is exercising royal prerogative similar to that of other kings and queens of the ancient Near East, including David and Solomon. Their example does not excuse her action but rather gives it perspective. Finally, she and Elijah clash over the most important theological question of the ninth century (and other centuries as well): Who is God in Israel? Elijah is victorious in the struggle. Yahweh is God in Israel.

CONTINUING THE CONVERSATION

By Jaime L. Waters

Jezebel: Examining the Roots of a Stereotype

Calling Jezebel a ruthless queen is not an exaggeration. The biblical tradition records Jezebel leading attacks against Israelite prophets, most notably Elijah. She is described as orchestrating both land seizure and murder before she dies a gruesome death. The biblical authors are certainly not fans of Jezebel; they reveal their hostility and biases in their extreme portrayals. As readers, it will be helpful for us to recognize the intentions of the biblical authors. Their portrait of Jezebel is deliberately and exclusively negative, which likely means she was effective in promoting her own faith tradition, perhaps over and above faith in the God of Israel.

Jezebel's Power

One of the negative narratives concerning Jezebel is her role in orchestrating the seizure of Naboth's vineyard and her involvement in his murder. When Nowell describes Jezebel's action, she questions whether Jezebel understands the significance of land in ancient Israel, maintaining that Jezebel "does not understand the importance of land to the Israelite. She does not know the significance of land as a sign of participation in the covenant. Thus she cannot understand Naboth's insistence on keeping his vineyard." The biblical text, however, does not suggest a lack of understanding on Jezebel's part. Rather, Jezebel might lack respect for Naboth's kinship ties to the land. Jezebel sees the land simply as something that can be commandeered by royal power.

The narratives about Jezebel are especially concerned with power. Feminist biblical scholars are frequently concerned about power dynamics that are evident in texts in which women are central characters. Jezebel, as queen of Israel, wields power and acts when her husband Ahab does not. Jezebel seems much more concerned about Ahab's weakness and inaction than about the significance of land to Israelites. She recognizes that Naboth's resistance to Ahab's power reflects badly on the monarchy in Israel. Jezebel's manipulative powerplays cost Naboth his land and life but enable the royal couple to maintain authority within the kingdom. Ultimately, their actions lead to their downfall and Jezebel's gruesome death.

The tradition surrounding Naboth's vineyard reveals that Jezebel's involvement was known by some in Israel. Jezebel sends a letter in Ahab's name, setting up Naboth and ordering his death. The officials followed the order, and when Naboth had been killed, "they sent word to Jezebel: 'Naboth has been stoned to death'" (1 Kgs 21:14). Although the order was sent in Ahab's name, the results were returned to Jezebel rather than Ahab. This suggests that the officials recognized Jezebel's power in the marriage and in the monarchy.

The "Jezebel" Stereotype

In later traditions, Jezebel's name becomes associated with sexual immorality, although the biblical traditions of 1–2 Kings are not related to sexual activity. In the biblical texts, Jezebel is associated with worship of Canaanite gods, hostility towards Israelite prophets, and abuse of power. Her name may have become associated with sexual activity because worship of other gods, which she promoted, was sometimes characterized metaphorically using language of adultery, infidelity, and prostitution (see, for example, 2 Kgs 9:22). By promoting worship of other gods, Jezebel encouraged the people of Israel to "cheat" on God with other "lovers" (gods) by making offerings to gods such as Baal and

Asherah. Although her sexual activity is not at issue, the sexualized language for apostasy (renouncing one's own god or religion) is connected with Jezebel's name and legacy.

In the New Testament, Jezebel's name is invoked in the context of offering food to idols, showing that she was remembered for encouraging unsanctioned cultic actions. The reference is couched in sexual terms as people are described as "play[ing] the harlot" and "eat[ing] food sacrificed to idols" (Rev 2:20-21).

Post-biblical tradition draws on these texts but emphasizes the sexualized language while disconnecting it from worship of other gods. Jezebel's name becomes an epithet associated with sexual immorality. Unfortunately, the label "Jezebel," detached from the historical Jezebel, has also been used in racialized and racist ways, as it has become a stereotype against African American women, associating us with promiscuity and sexual temptation. As an African American woman and biblical scholar, I have intersecting disdain for this action. It goes without saying that racist and sexist stereotypes should be avoided. Moreover, the roots of the Jezebel stereotype are flawed and fail to see metaphor in the biblical tradition.

As interpreters today, we can move beyond such interpretations and instead wrestle with the character of Jezebel in a thoughtful way. She might be a ruthless queen worthy of critique. Her name might rightfully be associated with corruption, religious suppression, and abuse of power. But it is time to drop Jezebel's association with sexual promiscuity.

EXPLORING LESSON ONE

1. What are Michal's feelings for David at the time of their marriage (1 Sam 18:28; 19:11), and why do her feelings seem to change later (2 Sam 6:16-23)? How is she treated by her father Saul and her husband David (1 Sam 18:21; 19:17; 2 Sam 6:21-23)?

_____

_____

_____

_____

_____

2. What defense would Bathsheba have had against the advances of King David (2 Sam 11:4)? (For an additional understanding of the authority of kings at this time in history, see 1 Sam 8:10-17.) Where might we still see this kind of imbalance of power in our world today?

_____

_____

_____

_____

_____

3. In ancient Jewish law, what consequences awaited those caught in adultery? (See Lev 20:10; Deut 22:22.)

_____

_____

_____

_____

4. How does the story in 1 Kings 1:11–2:20 illustrate that Bathsheba did, in the end, wield power and influence?

_____

_____

_____

_____

_____

5. Tamar is put in a vulnerable situation because of her brother's deception (2 Sam 13:1-6). An argument could be made that he not only deceived his sister and his father, but that he deceived himself. Can you think of situations where self-deception has led to harmful consequences?

_____

_____

_____

_____

_____

6. Which parts of the story of Tamar indicate that she was fighting to maintain her dignity in the face of cultural perceptions of women who were raped (2 Sam 13:7-20)?

_____

_____

_____

_____

_____

7. The queen of Sheba, a foreigner, recognizes Solomon's wisdom and leadership as gifts from the Lord and signs of God's favor and presence (1 Kgs 10:6-9). Why would her opinion have mattered to him or to his nation?

_____

_____

_____

_____

_____

8. a) The story of Jezebel and Ahab in 1 Kings highlights the fact that Israel struggled with God's command centuries earlier: "You shall not have other gods beside me . . . you shall not bow down before them or serve them" (Exod 20:3, 5). What factors might have made monotheism so challenging to Israel?

_____

_____

_____

_____

_____

b) Why do you suppose Jezebel has shouldered much of the blame over the centuries for Israel's infidelity? How does she misuse her position of power?

_____

_____

_____

_____

_____

9. Continuing the Conversation (see pp. 32–33): What is one possible explanation for how the name "Jezebel" came to be associated with sexual promiscuity?

_____

_____

_____

_____

_____

CLOSING PRAYER

Prayer

[Bathsheba] sent a message to inform David, "I am pregnant."   (2 Sam 11:5)

O God, just as Bathsheba was afforded few words and even fewer options, there are many in our world whose voices go unheard. Give us the courage to listen intently to those whose status makes them vulnerable, especially . . .

LESSON TWO

Women in the Image of God

Begin your personal study and group discussion with a simple and sincere prayer such as:

Prayer

You, O God, fill your people with courage, wisdom, and humility. Inspire us, as you inspired the women of Scripture, to use these virtues to transform the world.

Read pages 38–52, Lesson Two.

Respond to the questions on pages 53–55, Exploring Lesson Two.

The Closing Prayer on page 56 is for your personal use and may be used at the end of group discussion.

WOMEN IN THE IMAGE OF GOD

Scripture excerpts are found in shaded text boxes throughout the lesson. For additional context, you may wish to read all of the following in your Bible: Genesis 1–3; Proverbs 8–9; 31:10-31; Sirach 1; 24; 51; Wisdom 7–9.

The women portrayed in the preceding lessons are figures in Israel's history from the time of Abraham to the time of the kings. During the periods of the divided monarchy and the Babylonian exile, Israel began to consider wider issues: How did the world come to be? Where did the other nations come from? What can be said about human nature? Who is man? Who is woman? What can be said about the nature of God? How can one describe the relationship between God and human beings? The opening chapters of the book of Genesis represent Israel's reflection on these questions.

Israel's sages deepened this reflection on human nature and the nature of God. They described the bridge uniting God and human beings as wisdom. The image they used for God's wisdom is the image of woman. The portrayal of Woman Wisdom is found in the books of Proverbs, Sirach (Ecclesiasticus), and the Wisdom of Solomon.

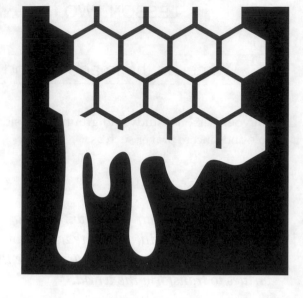

> Have dominion over the fish of the sea, the birds of the air, and all the living things that crawl on the earth. ²⁹God also said: See, I give you every seed-bearing plant on all the earth and every tree that has seed-bearing fruit on it to be your food; ³⁰and to all the wild animals, all the birds of the air, and all the living creatures that crawl on the earth, I give all the green plants for food. And so it happened. ³¹God looked at everything he had made, and found it very good. Evening came, and morning followed—the sixth day.

THE GENESIS IDEAL

Creation

> **Genesis 1:26-31**
>
> ²⁶Then God said: Let us make human beings in our image, after our likeness. Let them have dominion over the fish of the sea, the birds of the air, the tame animals, all the wild animals, and all the creatures that crawl on the earth.
>
> ²⁷God created mankind in his image;
> in the image of God he created them;
> male and female he created them.
>
> ²⁸God blessed them and God said to them: Be fertile and multiply; fill the earth and subdue it.

The story of creation that opens the book of Genesis is a major theological work. Genesis 1 was written by the final editor as an introduction to the whole Pentateuch (Genesis through Deuteronomy). It presents an image of God, a description of all other reality known to the author, and the relationship of God to this great world and its inhabitants. God is powerful and commanding, creating everything by a word. First God creates space and time—day and night, sky and earth, land and sea (1:3-10)—and then all those things that exist within space and time (1:11-31). Then God rests. All things are in order: each in its proper place, each in proper relationship to the other. Everything that God has created is good.

Then, God makes human beings: "Let us make *'adam* in our image, after our likeness" (1:26). The Hebrew word *'adam* is the generic term meaning "human" or "humanity." God creates all humanity and every human being in the divine image and likeness. Male and female are created by God in the divine image (1:27).

Because human beings are in God's image, they share God's life and power. This sharing of divine life is what blessing means. God gives them authority and responsibility over all other creation (1:26, 28). They become the channel through which God's lifegiving love comes to every other creature.

The Hebrew word **kabash** (**subdue**) frequently appears in contexts of war (e.g., 2 Sam 8:11; 2 Chr 28:10) or in situations where one person has power over another (e.g., Esth 7:8). Here, in the first chapter of Genesis (1:28), humans are given power over other created beings, a power that Pope St. John Paul II interprets as responsibility (*The Ecological Crisis*, 3). Rather than viewing humans as the center of creation with a right to dominate the rest of creation, the church recognizes that all created reality has integrity and intrinsic value as the sphere of God's action. The *Catechism of the Catholic Church* teaches that humans must "respect the particular goodness of every creature, to avoid any disordered use of things which would be in contempt of the Creator and would bring disastrous consequences for human beings and their environment" (339).

God also gives human beings power to continue creation through their sexuality (1:28). God entrusts them with the care and continuance of all that exists.

The theology of Genesis 1 portrays human beings as living images of God, representatives of and witnesses to God's power over and love toward all creation. All humans bear this respon-

sibility and share this greatness. Women as well as men are made in the image of God and bring God's touch to the world and its inhabitants. The Israelites were forbidden to make any images of God (Exod 20:4). They already had images of God in their lives: each other. St. Irenaeus, a second-century theologian, said that "the glory of God is the human being fully alive."

EVE

Another Reflection on Creation

Genesis 2:21-25

[21]So the LORD God cast a deep sleep on the man, and while he was asleep, he took out one of his ribs and closed up its place with flesh. [22]The LORD God then built the rib that he had taken from the man into a woman. When he brought her to the man, [23]the man said:

"This one, at last, is bone of my bones
    and flesh of my flesh;
This one shall be called 'woman,'
    for out of man this one has been taken."

[24]That is why a man leaves his father and mother and clings to his wife, and the two of them become one body.

[25]The man and his wife were both naked, yet they felt no shame.

Gen 2:4-25 is an older story of creation, although it appears second in the biblical text. The first story (Gen 1:1–2:3) describes God's creation of the cosmos. This second story focuses on the creation of and relationship between human beings and the natural world.

This creation story begins with the creation of *ha'adam*, the human (2:7). The Lord God forms the human creature out of the clay of the ground, *ha'adamah*, showing linguistic, metaphorical, and theological connections between humanity and the earth. The word *'adam* gives no indication of gender for this human creature throughout the chapter—the planting of the garden, the command not to eat of the tree, the creation of the animals—until God's creation of the second human being.

The Lord God casts a deep sleep over the first human and divides its flesh to create the second human: "The Lᴏʀᴅ God then built up into a woman (*'ishshah*) the rib that he had taken from the human (*ha'adam*)" (2:22, my translation). The close relationship between the first humans is emphasized: they are of the same flesh, and they cling to one another.

Just as male and female humans are created together in the image of God in Genesis 1, so in Genesis 2 man and woman are created to help one another, suggesting that God, in great wisdom, wants human beings to be in relationships with one another. The end of this creation story speaks of their nakedness, which will take on symbolic meaning in the following chapter.

Trouble in the Garden

Genesis 3:1-7

[1]Now the snake was the most cunning of all the wild animals that the Lᴏʀᴅ God had made. He asked the woman, "Did God really say, 'You shall not eat from any of the trees in the garden'?" [2]The woman answered the snake: "We may eat of the fruit of the trees in the garden; [3]it is only about the fruit of the tree in the middle of the garden that God said, 'You shall not eat it or even touch it, or else you will die.'" [4]But the snake said to the woman: "You certainly will not die! [5]God knows well that when you eat of it your eyes will be opened and you will be like gods, who know good and evil." [6]The woman saw that the tree was good for food and pleasing to the eyes, and the tree was desirable for gaining wisdom. So she took some of its fruit and ate it; and she also gave some to her husband, who was with her, and he ate it. [7]Then the eyes of both of them were opened, and they knew that they were naked; so they sewed fig leaves together and made loincloths for themselves.

The idyllic situation in the garden has become complex and imperfect. Man and woman have been forbidden to eat from the tree of the knowledge of good and evil. To eat from the tree is to know and experience both good and bad. To begin to know good and bad is to transition from infancy to the dawning awareness of childhood or from childhood to adulthood.[2] To know good and bad is to be wise.[3] To know good and bad is to be like God.

The serpent, cleverest of all the animals God made (3:1), points this out to the man and the woman. The two are together when the serpent speaks (3:6), although only the woman responds. The serpent attempts to drive a wedge between the humans and God by suggesting that God is keeping them from all the good things in the garden. The woman knows this is not true; only one tree is forbidden. She, however, suggests that they may not even touch it.

The serpent then focuses on the forbidden tree, the tree of the knowledge of good and evil. The serpent, in a classic portrayal of temptation, speaks the truth but deceives through it. The serpent makes three points: (1) you will not die; (2) your eyes will be opened; (3) you will be like God (or gods—the Hebrew word is the same for both).

You will not die: The implication in 2:17 is that death will follow immediately upon eating from the tree. It is true that the two do not die immediately, but death will eventually come to them.

Your eyes will be opened: Their eyes are opened to see first their own vulnerability, their nakedness (3:7), and then to see the ever-widening set of choices between good and bad.

You will be like God: In knowing the difference between good and bad, the man and woman are indeed like God (cf. 2 Sam 14:17). They glimpse part of what God knows, but in turning away from God, they have turned away from their source of life. They have threatened their greatest good, the breath of God which is their life (cf. Gen 2:7). They have opened themselves to their worst possibility, death.

God confirms the truth of the serpent's words: "See! The man has become like one of us, knowing good and evil! Now, what if he also reaches out his hand to take fruit from the tree of life, and eats of it and lives forever?" (3:22).

Both the man and the woman are present to hear the serpent's words. Both make the choice. Both eat from the tree. Both are told by God that their share in God's life and power, their capacity for fruitfulness, is damaged. The woman will suffer in pregnancy and childbirth: "I will intensify your toil in childbearing; / in pain you shall bring forth children" (3:16). Most translations obscure the fact that there are three terms in 3:16: "hard work," "pregnancies," "bear children." The verse literally reads: "I will increase your hard work and your pregnancies; with labor shall you bear children." The term for "hard work" or "toil" (*issabon*) appears also in 3:17, addressed to the man: "In toil you shall eat its [the ground's] yield / all the days of your life." The man will suffer in bringing forth food from the earth. Both will have to labor as they participate in the process of creation.

The story of Genesis 2–3 ends in ambiguity. The man names the woman Eve, which in Hebrew sounds like "life," because she is the mother of all the living (3:20). The Lord God takes pity on the pair and makes leather garments for them (3:21). But God also banishes them from the garden and bars the way to the tree of life (3:23-24).

Woman and man share the same flesh, breathe the same breath. Woman and man are both responsible for breaking the bond with God, for bringing into human life the knowledge of both good and bad. Woman and man will each suffer death. Together, woman and man continue the blessing, even with struggle, of perpetuating life in the world.

WISDOM (HEBREW *HOKMAH*, GREEK *SOPHIA*)

Street Preacher

> ### Proverbs 8:1-3
>
> ¹Does not Wisdom call,
>   and Understanding raise her voice?
> ²On the top of the heights along the road,
>   at the crossroads she takes her stand;
> ³By the gates at the approaches of the city,
>   in the entryways she cries aloud.

In the first chapters of the book of Proverbs, a female figure appears who is the personification of the wisdom of God. In the biblical text, she is simply called "Wisdom" (*Hokmah*), although many scholars refer to this figure as "Woman Wisdom" to highlight that grammatically and literarily, Wisdom is female.[4]

Woman Wisdom appears first as a prophet, a street preacher. She cries out at street corners and at the place of business, the city gates (see 1:20-21). She has a message for human beings. She offers to pour out her spirit upon them (1:23). She promises instruction better than silver, and knowledge better than gold (8:10). She is the source and strength of all the good things human beings do (8:12-16) and the provider of all the good things they enjoy (8:17-21). Who is this Woman Wisdom?

Adam and Eve hide from God (Gen 3:8). Julius Schnorr von Carolsfeld (1860)

God's Firstborn

Proverbs 8:22-31

²²"The LORD begot me, the beginning of his
works,
the forerunner of his deeds of long ago;
²³From of old I was formed,
at the first, before the earth.
²⁴When there were no deeps I was brought
forth,
when there were no fountains or springs
of water;
²⁵Before the mountains were settled into
place,
before the hills, I was brought forth;
²⁶When the earth and the fields were not yet
made,
nor the first clods of the world.
²⁷When he established the heavens, there
was I,
when he marked out the vault over the
face of the deep;
²⁸When he made firm the skies above,
when he fixed fast the springs of the deep;
²⁹When he set for the sea its limit,
so that the waters should not transgress
his command;
When he fixed the foundations of earth,
³⁰then was I beside him as artisan;
I was his delight day by day,
playing before him all the while,
³¹Playing over the whole of his earth,
having my delight with human beings.

In Proverbs 8:22-31 Wisdom sings a hymn describing her origins and her relationship to God and to human beings. She is God's firstborn, begotten before creation, brought to birth before earth and sea. She was not only present when God created space and time and every creature—she was God's architect, the designer of God's creation. Through her all things were created.

The final verses of this section (8:30-31) capture the reason for her great worth: She is the bridge between God and human beings. Two key words illustrate this function: "delight" and "play." Wisdom is God's delight; she finds delight in human beings. She plays before God; she plays on the earth. She lives among the human and the divine. Her signature, the way she can be recognized, is in play and delight. Through these two characteristics she joins God with humankind. Because of this function, all good things come through her.

 Wisdom's description of herself in Proverbs 8:30-31 takes a poetic form called a **chiasm**, from the Greek letter *chi* that looks like an X. Drawing a line between the repeated words "delight" and "playing" forms an X:

I was his delight day by day,	playing before him all the while.
Playing over the whole of his earth,	having my delight with human beings.

The chapter closes with Wisdom's exhortation (8:32-36). Again she calls to people to listen to her. Two beatitudes describe those who heed:

Now, children, listen to me;
happy are they who keep my ways.
Happy the one who listens to me,
attending daily at my gates,
keeping watch at my doorposts. (8:32, 34)

Why are they happy? Because those who find Wisdom find life and God's favor (8:35). In contrast, those who "miss" her (NABRE: "pass [her] by") harm their lives (8:36). The word "miss" comes from the common Hebrew word for sin. To sin in Hebrew is literally "to miss the mark." To "miss" or "pass by" Wisdom is equivalent to sin, which brings death. Those who hate Wisdom love death (8:36).

The Banquet

> ### Proverbs 9:1-5
>
> [1]Wisdom has built her house,
>   she has set up her seven columns;
> [2]She has prepared her meat, mixed her wine,
>   yes, she has spread her table.
> [3]She has sent out her maidservants; she calls
>   from the heights out over the city:
> [4]"Let whoever is naive turn in here;
>   to any who lack sense I say,
> [5]Come, eat of my food,
>   and drink of the wine I have mixed!"

Woman Wisdom has called out to people. Now she prepares the banquet to which she invites them. She builds her house: the world. She sets up seven columns: the perfect number; her house will not fall. She prepares the meat, mixes the wine, sets the table, sends out the invitations. Everything is in readiness. This offer of food and drink is an offer to partake of Wisdom herself. We have a saying: "You are what you eat." Wisdom says, "Eat of me and you will have life" (see 9:5-6, 11).

In Proverbs 3:18 Wisdom is described as the tree of life. In Genesis 2–3 the tree of life is at the center of the garden. Those who eat of it will live forever (see Gen 3:22). After the man and the woman ate from the tree of the knowledge of good and evil, God set a guard on the way to the tree of life (Gen 3:24). Now Wisdom proclaims that she is that tree of life. The gift of life is offered again. This food is not prohibited for human beings. On the contrary, people are exhorted to come, eat, and drink. Those who partake of Wisdom find life.

Another female figure, Folly, is described in the introductory section of Proverbs (chs. 1–9). In chapter nine she also invites the simple to come and eat at her house. She, too, calls from the city heights. Her invitation sounds deceptively like the invitation of Wisdom:

> "Let those who are naive turn in here,
>   to those who lack sense I say,
> Stolen water is sweet,
>   and bread taken secretly is pleasing!" (9:16-17)

But her food is not truth and discipline. She offers deceit and wanton pleasure. The consequence of eating at her table is not life but death, for "her guests are in the depths of Sheol" (9:18). In contrast to Woman Wisdom, Woman Folly never appears again. She herself disappears into the nether world.

God holding compasses at the creation of the world, like an artisan.
Bible Historiale *(c. 1411)*

The introductory section of Proverbs (chs. 1–9) is framed by an inclusion (the same phrase at beginning and end): "Fear of the LORD is the beginning of knowledge" (1:7) and "the beginning of wisdom is fear of the LORD" (9:10). Fear of the Lord is awe at the greatness of God and wonder that this great God loves and cares for us. Fear of the Lord is the realization that God is God, and we are not. Fear of the Lord leads to Woman Wisdom, and she leads to knowledge of God. To know God is to love God. Love of God leads to greater awe, greater fear of the Lord, greater wisdom. "Fear of the Lord" becomes another name for Woman Wisdom.

Wisdom as Wife

Proverbs 31:10-31

¹⁰Who can find a woman of worth?
Far beyond jewels is her value.
¹¹Her husband trusts her judgment;
he does not lack income.
¹²She brings him profit, not loss,
all the days of her life.
¹³She seeks out wool and flax
and weaves with skillful hands.
¹⁴Like a merchant fleet,
she secures her provisions from afar.
¹⁵She rises while it is still night,
and distributes food to her household,
a portion to her maidservants.
¹⁶She picks out a field and acquires it;
from her earnings she plants a vineyard.
¹⁷She girds herself with strength;
she exerts her arms with vigor.
¹⁸She enjoys the profit from her dealings;
her lamp is never extinguished at night.
¹⁹She puts her hands to the distaff,
and her fingers ply the spindle.
²⁰She reaches out her hands to the poor,
and extends her arms to the needy.
²¹She is not concerned for her household
when it snows—

all her charges are doubly clothed.
²²She makes her own coverlets;
fine linen and purple are her clothing.
²³Her husband is prominent at the city gates
as he sits with the elders of the land.
²⁴She makes garments and sells them,
and stocks the merchants with belts.
²⁵She is clothed with strength and dignity,
and laughs at the days to come.
²⁶She opens her mouth in wisdom;
kindly instruction is on her tongue.
²⁷She watches over the affairs of her household,
and does not eat the bread of idleness.
²⁸Her children rise up and call her blessed;
her husband, too, praises her:
²⁹"Many are the women of proven worth,
but you have excelled them all."
³⁰Charm is deceptive and beauty fleeting;
the woman who fears the LORD is to be praised.
³¹Acclaim her for the work of her hands,
and let her deeds praise her at the city gates.

The book of Proverbs ends with an acrostic poem of 22 lines. In an acrostic (or alphabetic) poem, each verse begins with the next letter of the Hebrew alphabet. Most acrostics are twenty-two lines, corresponding to the twenty-two letters of the Hebrew alphabet.

This is a poem in praise of the "woman of worth," the woman who has the strength (*hayil*) of a military man or the resources (*hayil*) of the wealthy. The virtues of this woman are overwhelming. She spins; she weaves; she makes clothes. She buys fields; she sells garments; she plants a vineyard with her profits. She takes care not only of her own household, but also of the poor and needy. She teaches wisdom. Her husband and children can do nothing but praise her.

Who is this woman who cares for everything and everyone? Is she not Wisdom? At the beginning of the book of Proverbs the young man was counseled to seek Wisdom, to court her, to do anything he could to obtain her. At the end of the book is a description of the happiness of the one who has taken Wisdom into his house and lives with her. This woman, whose name is "Fear of the Lord" (see 31:30), will bring him the delights of life through all his days. Proverbs ends with the happiness of the one who finds Woman Wisdom.

Word of God / Breath of God

The book of Sirach was written in Hebrew and then translated into Greek. At the end of the first century CE, when the Jewish community made a final decision on which books would be included in the Hebrew Bible, the book of Sirach was not included. Christians, however, continued to use it in the Greek translation.

At the time of the Reformation, Protestant Christians began using only the books included in the Hebrew Bible. Roman Catholic Christians continued using other books from the Greek Bible, including the book of Sirach. Note that there are several numbering systems for chapters and verses in the book of Sirach because of the complexity of its textual tradition. The verse numbers indicated here are those found in the NABRE.

The book of Sirach is constructed on three great pillars, three hymns to Wisdom, found in chapters 1, 24, and 51:13-30. Ben Sira introduces his discussion of Woman Wisdom by echoing Proverbs 8: Wisdom comes from God and was created by God. It is God who knows her and pours her forth upon the world (Sir 1:1-10). Then the sage sings a hymn to Wisdom as Fear of the Lord (1:11-30). Fear of the Lord is the beginning, the fullness, the garland, and the root of Wisdom. Fear of the Lord (i.e., Wisdom) brings all good things to those who live by her.

Chapter 24, like Proverbs 8, contains a hymn of self-praise sung by Wisdom in which she describes herself, her origins, her relationship to God, and the good things she does for human beings:

More Women of the Old Testament

The "Wailing Women" in Jeremiah

A powerful connection between women and wisdom is found in Jeremiah 9:16-21. The context is a time of destruction, war, and suffering. During this traumatic period, God instructs Jeremiah to call the mourning women, the wise women, to lift up a lament for the community: "Inquire, and call the wailing women to come; / summon the most skilled of them" (9:16). The reference to these women as "skilled" indicates that this task was a profession or a guild, but the word is a form of *hokmah*, meaning "wisdom." The wise mourning women are summoned because they recognize the realities of war and publicly give voice to suffering. Similar to Miriam and the women leading a liturgical commemoration after the exodus, the wailing women in Jeremiah lead a liturgical lamentation in response to human disobedience to the covenant, suffering, and death. The women are told, "Teach your daughters a dirge, / and each other a lament" (9:19). This injunction incorporates generations of women into the ritual mourning, preparing them for liturgical leadership and ensuring that the larger community will continue to articulate its grief.

—*Jaime L. Waters*

Sirach 24:1-33

¹Wisdom sings her own praises,
   among her own people she proclaims her
      glory.
²In the assembly of the Most High she opens
      her mouth,
   in the presence of his host she tells of her
      glory:
³"From the mouth of the Most High I came
      forth,
   and covered the earth like a mist.
⁴In the heights of heaven I dwelt,
   and my throne was in a pillar of cloud.
⁵The vault of heaven I compassed alone,
   and walked through the deep abyss.
⁶Over waves of the sea, over all the land,
   over every people and nation I held sway.
⁷Among all these I sought a resting place.
   In whose inheritance should I abide?
⁸"Then the Creator of all gave me his
      command,
   and my Creator chose the spot for my
      tent.
He said, 'In Jacob make your dwelling,
   in Israel your inheritance.'
⁹Before all ages, from the beginning, he
      created me,
   and through all ages I shall not cease to be.
¹⁰In the holy tent I ministered before him,
   and so I was established in Zion.
¹¹In the city he loves as he loves me, he gave
      me rest;
   in Jerusalem, my domain.
¹²I struck root among the glorious people,
   in the portion of the Lord, his heritage.
¹³"Like a cedar in Lebanon I grew tall,
   like a cypress on Mount Hermon;
¹⁴I grew tall like a palm tree in Engedi,
   like rosebushes in Jericho;
Like a fair olive tree in the field,
   like a plane tree beside water I grew tall.
¹⁵Like cinnamon and fragrant cane,
   like precious myrrh I gave forth perfume;
Like galbanum and onycha and mastic,
   like the odor of incense in the holy tent.

¹⁶"I spread out my branches like a terebinth,
   my branches so glorious and so graceful.
¹⁷I bud forth delights like a vine;
   my blossoms are glorious and rich fruit.
¹⁹Come to me, all who desire me,
   and be filled with my fruits.
²⁰You will remember me as sweeter than
      honey,
   better to have than the honeycomb.
²¹Those who eat of me will hunger still,
   those who drink of me will thirst for more.
²²Whoever obeys me will not be put to
      shame,
   and those who serve me will never go
      astray."
²³All this is the book of the covenant of the
      Most High God,
   the Law which Moses commanded us
   as a heritage for the community of Jacob.
²⁵It overflows, like the Pishon, with wisdom,
   and like the Tigris at the time of first
      fruits.
²⁶It runs over, like the Euphrates, with
      understanding,
   and like the Jordan at harvest time.
²⁷It floods like the Nile with instruction,
   like the Gihon at vintage time.
²⁸The first human being never finished
      comprehending wisdom,
   nor will the last succeed in fathoming her.
²⁹For deeper than the sea are her thoughts,
   and her counsels, than the great abyss.
³⁰Now I, like a stream from a river,
   and like water channeling into a garden—
³¹I said, "I will water my plants,
   I will drench my flower beds."
Then suddenly this stream of mine became a
      river,
   and this river of mine became a sea.
³²Again I will make my teachings shine forth
      like the dawn;
   I will spread their brightness afar off.
³³Again I will pour out instruction like
      prophecy
   and bestow it on generations yet to come.

Wisdom begins by describing her origins (24:3-7). She came from the mouth of the Most High. She is God's Word, God's Breath/Spirit. As the spirit/wind that hovered over the waters (Gen 1:2) and the mist/stream that covered the earth at the beginning (Gen 2:6), she is present at creation. She is universal; she is everywhere. Still, she seeks a place to live, a place to rest. Her place, chosen for her by God, is in Jerusalem with God's covenant people (24:8-12). There she pitches her tent; there she ministers before God in the holy tent, the temple. She is available to all people, but she lives with Israel.

The image of Wisdom as a tree echoes Proverbs (Sir 24:12-17; cf. Prov 3:18). She strikes root among God's people. She is like every beautiful tree—cedar, cypress, palm, olive. She is found everywhere from the north to the south (Lebanon to Jericho), from the mountains to the desert (Mount Hermon to Engedi). She offers everything pleasant to smell, see, and taste—cedar, roses, cinnamon, grapes. She feeds all who long for her (24:19-21). Her food is sweeter than honey; her food is herself! All who eat of her will hunger still, who drink of her will thirst for more. One will never be able to get enough. What she offers is life.

She concludes her song in verse 22 with a promise similar to Proverbs 8:35-36. Those who obey her will not be shamed; those who serve her will not fall short or "go astray." The word here is again related to the common Hebrew word for sin, i.e., to "miss the mark."

Ben Sira breaks new ground with his next statement: "All this is the book of the covenant of the Most High God, / the Law which Moses commanded us / as a heritage for the community of Jacob" (24:23). Woman Wisdom, who is God's Word, God's Spirit, is the Torah. She lives in Israel. Where she is to be found is in the Book of the Law, the Sacred Scripture of God's people. She is God's revelation of self, the word of God in human words. She is present to anyone who meditates upon this book.

Ben Sira then compares Wisdom to the water of life (24:25-29). He echoes Gen 2:10-14, the description of the four rivers that water the whole earth. To the Genesis list of the Pishon, Gihon, Tigris, and Euphrates, he adds the other rivers of Israel's experience: the Jordan and the Nile. As these rivers give life to all creation, so Woman Wisdom gives life. No human being will ever exhaust Wisdom's gifts. She is deeper even than the sea, the abyss of primeval chaos (Gen 1:2). She is God's gift to human beings who have an infinite thirst for truth and love (Sir 24:21).

Wisdom can never be totally comprehended by human beings, but Ben Sira does not consider her inaccessible. In a profound description of the role of the teacher, Ben Sira describes his own work (24:30-33). He digs a little channel from Wisdom's stream in order to water his garden. But no teacher can measure the power of Wisdom flowing out through teaching. The little channel becomes a river; the river becomes a sea. Every teacher labors, not only for the present time, but for every generation to come. Wisdom, who is found in reflection on common human experience, is available to everyone. But the teacher has special responsibility to keep Wisdom's river clear and flowing.

Wisdom as Bride

Sirach 51:13-30

[13]When I was young and innocent,
  I sought wisdom.
[14]She came to me in her beauty,
  and until the end I will cultivate her.
[15]As the blossoms yielded to ripening grapes,
  the heart's joy,
My feet kept to the level path
  because from earliest youth I was familiar with her.
[16]In the short time I paid heed,
  I met with great instruction.
[17]Since in this way I have profited,
  I will give my Teacher grateful praise.

continue

¹⁸I resolved to tread her paths;
  I have been jealous for the good and will
    not turn back.
¹⁹I burned with desire for her,
  never relenting.
I became preoccupied with her,
  never weary of extolling her.
I spread out my hands to the heavens
  and I came to know her secrets.
²⁰For her I purified my hands;
  in cleanness I attained to her.
At first acquaintance with her, I gained
    understanding
  such that I will never forsake her.
²¹My whole being was stirred to seek her;
  therefore I have made her my prize
    possession.
²²The LORD has rewarded me with lips,
  with a tongue for praising him.
²³Come aside to me, you untutored,
  and take up lodging in the house of
    instruction;
²⁴How long will you deprive yourself of
    wisdom's food,
  how long endure such bitter thirst?
²⁵I open my mouth and speak of her:
  gain wisdom for yourselves at no cost.
²⁶Take her yoke upon your neck;
  that your mind may receive her teaching.
For she is close to those who seek her,
  and the one who is in earnest finds her.
²⁷See for yourselves! I have labored only a little,
  but have found much.
²⁸Acquire but a little instruction,
  and you will win silver and gold through her.
²⁹May your soul rejoice in God's mercy;
  do not be ashamed to give him praise.
³⁰Work at your tasks in due season,
  and in his own time God will give you
    your reward.

Like Proverbs, the book of Sirach ends with an acrostic poem. This is a song of rejoicing, a passionate love song, from one who has found Wisdom. In the first half the author describes his own experience. He sought Woman Wisdom as a young man. He pursued her with devotion. He courted her with burning desire. He cleansed his whole life for her. She came to him in beauty, stirring the center of his being. She became the subject of his every thought, the goal of his whole life.

In the second half of the poem (51:23-30), Ben Sira makes an offer to other young men. If they will come to his school, they, too, will gain what he has found. Wisdom will satisfy their hunger and thirst. She will bring them silver and gold. She is the gift of God.

Image of God

Wisdom 7:22–8:1

²²Wisdom, the artisan of all, taught me.
For in her is a spirit
  intelligent, holy, unique,
Manifold, subtle, agile,
  clear, unstained, certain,
Never harmful, loving the good, keen,
  ²³unhampered, beneficent, kindly,
Firm, secure, tranquil,
  all-powerful, all-seeing,
And pervading all spirits,
  though they be intelligent, pure and very
    subtle.
²⁴For Wisdom is mobile beyond all motion,
  and she penetrates and pervades all things
    by reason of her purity.
²⁵For she is a breath of the might of God
  and a pure emanation of the glory of the
    Almighty;
  therefore nothing defiled can enter into her.
²⁶For she is the reflection of eternal light,
  the spotless mirror of the power of God,
  the image of his goodness.
²⁷Although she is one, she can do all things,
  and she renews everything while herself
    perduring;

> Passing into holy souls from age to age,
>   she produces friends of God and prophets.
> ²⁸For God loves nothing so much as the one
>   who dwells with Wisdom.
> ²⁹For she is fairer than the sun
>   and surpasses every constellation of the
>   stars.
> Compared to light, she is found more
>   radiant;
> ³⁰though night supplants light,
>   wickedness does not prevail over Wisdom.
> ⁸:¹Indeed, she spans the world from end to
>   end mightily
>   and governs all things well.

The description of Woman Wisdom in the Wisdom of Solomon is intense and dramatic. The Wisdom of Solomon was written in Greek. Like the book of Sirach, the Wisdom of Solomon was not included in the Hebrew Bible. Thus it is in the canon (list of books) of the Roman Catholic Bible but not Jewish and Protestant Bibles. Its author, a first-century sage, writes in the persona of Solomon. In Wisdom 6:22–9:18, he describes Solomon's experience with Woman Wisdom. After an introduction (6:22-25), there are two passages of Solomon's personal experience (7:1-22a; 8:2-21) which surround this ecstatic description of Wisdom herself (7:22b–8:1). The section then concludes with a prayer (9:1-18).

Solomon begins by promising to share everything he knows about Wisdom (6:22-25). He acknowledges that he is human like everyone else, born in the ordinary way (7:1-6). But he prayed and pleaded for Wisdom, recognizing that her value reduced everything else to dust (7:7-11). He rejoiced in Wisdom, the "mother" of all that is good (7:12). Here, in order to describe Woman Wisdom, the author of the book coins a new word in Greek, *genetis*, meaning "creator," "begetter," or "mother." The masculine term already existed, but the feminine term appears here for the first time.

Solomon promises to share Wisdom freely with everyone and prays to speak well of her (7:13-16). He credits Wisdom with giving him knowledge of all major areas of knowledge in Greek education: astronomy, physics, zoology, botany, and medicine (7:17-22a). All these things he learned because Wisdom, the craftswoman or artisan (*technitis*) of all, taught him (cf. Prov 8:30).

The excerpt here, the description of Wisdom (7:22b–8:1), begins with twenty-one characteristics of her spirit. Twenty-one is the product of two perfect numbers, three and seven. Wisdom is perfection multiplied by perfection. But that is not enough for her description. She is the motion of all that moves; she penetrates everything that exists. She is better than light. She rules all things. Most important, however, is her relationship to God and human beings.

This description of Wisdom's relationship to God is clearer and more intense than the descriptions found in Proverbs and Sirach. Wisdom is a breath of God's power, the outpouring of God's glory. She is the shining of God's light. She is the perfect reflection of God's power and goodness. She can do all things.

Wisdom's relationship to human beings is of great benefit to us. She fills the prophets with God's word. She is the one who makes us friends of God.

Solomon's testimony to his own experience both precedes (7:1-22a) and follows (8:2-21) this description of Wisdom. Solomon is the wise young man who seeks Woman Wisdom as a bride. She will teach him everything that he needs for a full life (8:2-8). She not only gives him joy and peace; because of her he will have immortality (8:9-16). The concept of immortality is grasped very late in the Old Testament period. The good news of immortality is most fully described in Wisdom. Here the author simply proclaims that this gift of immortality comes from Woman Wisdom (8:13). Wisdom herself is a gift of God. Therefore Solomon, who is set up as a model for all of us, seeks her with all his energy (8:17-21).

The section concludes with a prayer for the gift of Wisdom (9:1-18) which leads into a narration of Israel's history seen through the lens of Wisdom's power to save (10:1–19:22).

Conclusion

In the Wisdom books we find a personification of God's wisdom as a woman who is desirable and should be sought. The final chapters of Proverbs and Sirach present Wisdom as a wife. The person who has succeeded in winning her as a spouse is rewarded with all the goodness and delight that life can bring.

The book of Wisdom clarifies what Proverbs and Sirach have suggested. Woman Wisdom is an image of God. In speaking of her, we speak of God. Thus Woman Wisdom is Scripture's most powerful confirmation of creation's truth: "God created humankind in his image, in the image of God he created them; male and female he created them" (Gen 1:27, NRSV). Man is an image of God. Woman is an image of God. There is no superiority of one over the other as image. The two together are the best image of God in all of creation.

 Three substantial biblical texts describe **Wisdom (*Hokmah*)** in detail:

	Proverbs 8:22-36	**Sirach 24:1-29**	**Wisdom 7:22–8:1**
Who is she?	counselor of the Creator (8:30)	God's word (24:3); God's law (24:23)	pure image of God (7:25-27)
Where is she?	"at the crossroads" (8:1-3); before God and on the earth (8:30-31)	everywhere (24:4-6); lives in the holy city (24:8-12)	everywhere; "pervades all things" (7:24)
Relationship to God	God's child (8:22); God's delight (8:30)	word from God's mouth (24:3)	aura of God's might; outpouring of God's glory; shining of God's light; mirror of God's power; image of God's goodness (7:25-26)
Relationship to human beings	delights in them (8:31)	feeds them and makes them succeed (24:19-22)	makes them "friends of God and prophets" (7:27)
Relationship to the created world	present before and during creation (8:23-29); creation's designer (8:30)	like every sweet-smelling tree (24:13-17); like all refreshing water (24:25-29)	"renews everything" (7:27)
Her worth	more than gold and silver (8:19)	"sweeter" than honey (24:20)	"fairer than the sun" and surpasses the stars and all light (7:29-30)
Her offer/her gifts	riches, honor (8:18, 21); life and God's favor (8:35)	most desirable nourishment (24:19-21)	"all good things" and "countless riches" (7:11); immortality (8:13, 17)

CONTINUING THE CONVERSATION

By Jaime L. Waters

Woman Wisdom: Feminine Language for God

Proverbs 8 offers us a rich tradition about Woman Wisdom and her relationship to God and humanity. Irene Nowell treats verses 1-3 and 22-31. Let's take a look now at surrounding verses that contain additional insights worthy of our exploration.

Proverbs 8:4-9

The chapter begins by depicting Woman Wisdom going into the streets, raising her voice to address the community. Wisdom speaks to humanity boldly and loudly; Nowell characterizes her as a "street preacher." Her message comes through in the verses that follow:

4"To you, O people, I call;
  my appeal is to you mortals.
5You naive ones, gain prudence,
  you fools, gain sense.
6Listen! for noble things I speak;
  my lips proclaim honest words.
7Indeed, my mouth utters truth,
  and my lips abhor wickedness.
8All the words of my mouth are sincere,
  none of them wily or crooked;
9All of them are straightforward to the
    intelligent,
  and right to those who attain knowledge."

Woman Wisdom addresses people directly, and she calls them naive and foolish. The language is meant to inspire, although the designations are likely off-putting. Wisdom is depicted as wanting people to gain understanding so they can be wise like her. She exhorts humans to listen attentively because she speaks truthfully. There is an intensity in her address that shows the significance of wisdom in the world.

Proverbs 8:10-13

10"Take my instruction instead of silver,
  and knowledge rather than choice gold.
11[For Wisdom is better than corals,
  and no treasures can compare with her.]
12I, Wisdom, dwell with prudence,
  and useful knowledge I have.
13 [The fear of the LORD is hatred of evil;]
Pride, arrogance, the evil way,
  and the perverse mouth I hate."

As her address continues, Wisdom proclaims her worth as more valuable than the finest metals and stones. She also offers details on what "fear of the LORD" means. At the beginning of the book, the fear of the LORD is described as "the beginning of knowledge," and we are told that those who are foolish despise wisdom (1:7). In Proverbs 8, fear of the LORD is connected with hatred of evil, meaning that true wisdom involves seeking and doing what is good. Personifying wisdom as a woman who is valued and desirable is a way to encourage people to be persuaded of wisdom's importance in their lives. In Proverbs, living wisely and seeking wisdom are closely connected to living a righteous life.

Proverbs 8:14-21

14"Mine are counsel and advice;
  Mine is strength; I am understanding.
15By me kings reign,
  and rulers enact justice;
16By me princes govern,
  and nobles, all the judges of the earth.
17Those who love me I also love,
  and those who seek me find me.
18With me are riches and honor,
  wealth that endures, and righteousness.

19My fruit is better than gold, even pure gold,
and my yield than choice silver.
20On the way of righteousness I walk,
along the paths of justice,
21Granting wealth to those who love me,
and filling their treasuries."

In her exhortation, Wisdom declares her connection to justice. Wisdom proclaims that rulers should enact justice as part of their leadership, and she links just governance with wisdom. In these verses, we gain clarity on how Wisdom finds her way within humanity; it is especially evident in proper leadership that facilitates a just society. Once again, the value of wisdom is emphasized, as is the importance of finding strength and advice by thoughtfully engaging wisdom.

Wisdom then shares insights into her origins (8:22-31), discussed in your commentary. Here Woman Wisdom is depicted as created first and is a participant in the creative process with God.

Proverbs 8:34-36

34"Happy the one who listens to me,
attending daily at my gates,
keeping watch at my doorposts;

35For whoever finds me finds life,
and wins favor from the Lord;
36But those who pass me by do violence to
themselves;
all who hate me love death."

The end of Proverbs 8 reveals the consequences of not seeking wisdom: people harm themselves and draw closer to death. Wisdom is framed as something that enriches life and allows humanity to thrive, so the opposite actions can have negative consequences on humanity.

A Divine Attribute

The image of Woman Wisdom participating in creation and being present in humanity depicts wisdom as having divine origins and being divine presence within creation. Having such an explicit link between God and Woman Wisdom is ripe with interpretive possibilities. As much of the language we typically use for God is masculine, such as Father and Lord, Woman Wisdom as another divine attribute infuses biblically rooted feminine language into our vocabulary for God.

EXPLORING LESSON TWO

1. According to the commentary, what is the meaning of being made "in the image of God" (Gen 1:26-27)? What experiences have helped you believe you are an image of God? (See Ps 8:5-6; Wis 2:23; Sir 17:1.)

_____

_____

_____

_____

_____

2. How does knowledge of the Hebrew words *'adam* and *'ishshah* (Gen 2:21-23) enhance your understanding of the second account of creation?

_____

_____

_____

_____

3. Sometimes cultural biases creep into our interpretation and use of Scripture, as with the account of God creating man and woman (see 1 Cor 11:8-9; 1 Tim 2:13). How might we guard against misapplying God's word?

_____

_____

_____

_____

4. Do you ever find yourself wishing we had remained in the garden, unaware of the difference between good and evil (Gen 2:17; 3:5)? In your experience, what responsibility comes with such knowledge? (See Deut 30:19-20.)

_____

_____

_____

_____

_____

5. Eve is sometimes thought of as a temptress (Gen 3:6), but she is also given an exalted name that means "mother of all the living" (Gen 3:20). In your experience, is there a danger in painting another person with only one brush, focusing only on negative or even positive attributes?

_____

_____

_____

_____

_____

_____

6. What are some of the spiritual foods found at the table prepared by Wisdom (Prov 8:10-21; 9:2-5)? And what is found at Folly's table (Prov 9:13-18)?

_____

_____

_____

_____

_____

_____

7. What is an appropriate understanding of the phrase "fear of the Lord"? (See Ps 111:10; 130:4; Prov 1:7; 9:10; 14:27; Jer 10:7.)

_____

_____

_____

_____

8. In what ways have you sought wisdom? To what extent has your pursuit of wisdom matched your pursuit of success or other things (Sir 51:13-30; Prov 16:16)? Have you noticed changes in priorities in different periods of your life?

_____

_____

_____

_____

9. Review the characteristics of Wisdom listed in the book of Wisdom 7:22-24. Which of these characteristics is evident in your life? Which of Wisdom's characteristics do you most desire at this time in your life?

_____

_____

_____

_____

_____

10. Continuing the Conversation: The strong biblical connection between Woman Wisdom and God is "ripe with interpretive possibilities." In what ways does this biblically feminine language resonate with you, and in what ways do you find it challenging?

_____

_____

_____

_____

_____

_____

CLOSING PRAYER

Prayer

Passing into holy souls from age to age,
[Wisdom] produces friends of God and
*   prophets.   (Wis 7:27)*

Fill us with the nourishment of Wisdom, O God, so that our devotion to your way will produce fruit in our lives and in our communities. In word and deed may our friendship with you draw others to know you. And let us heed the words of prophets who remind us of our responsibility to further your kingdom. We pray for the gift of wise decisions, especially . . .

LESSON THREE

Women of Courage and Strength

Begin your personal study and group discussion with a simple and sincere prayer such as:

Prayer

You, O God, fill your people with courage, wisdom, and humility. Inspire us, as you inspired the women of Scripture, to use these virtues to transform the world.

Read pages 58–78, Lesson Three.

Respond to the questions on pages 79–81, Exploring Lesson Three.

The Closing Prayer on page 81 is for your personal use and may be used at the end of group discussion.

Scripture excerpts are found in shaded text boxes throughout the lesson.

WOMEN OF COURAGE AND STRENGTH

Two women whose stories are told in deutero-canonical books of the Old Testament (written in Greek and not included in Jewish and Protestant Bibles) bring biblical themes of faith, courage, beauty, and virtue into sharp focus. One woman is a virtuous widow and steely warrior; the other is a victim of male deceit who becomes an icon of trust in God's faithfulness. Both women are exemplars of the strength that derives from resolute faith in the God of Israel.

JUDITH

The Setting

In the first eight chapters of the book of Judith we learn of the distress of the people of a little Israelite town named Bethulia. In order to emphasize the magnitude of their danger, the author has lined up and joined together the greatest enemies of Israel throughout its history: the Assyrians, who took captive the ten tribes of the northern kingdom in 722 BCE, and Nebuchadnezzar, king of the Babylonians, who destroyed Jerusalem and exiled people of the southern kingdom in 587 BCE. These two peoples symbolize the greatest possible threat to God's people. This book indicates that the danger Judith's people face is as great as the danger of both of these powerful enemies combined.

The author of the book of Judith seems to have deliberately confused the historical characters. Nebuchadnezzar (actually king of the Babylonians) is portrayed as king of the Assyrians. In this story the Assyrian army, in the name of King Nebuchadnezzar and under the leadership of General Holofernes, has conquered the whole ancient Near East except the land of Judea.

By also confusing historical dates, the author gives us several clues that God's people are not so easily defeated. The year given in the story seems to apply to the Babylonian exile (587–539 BCE), not the Assyrian captivity, which began in 722 BCE. The book of Judith says that Nebuchadnezzar (identified as king of the Assyrians) began his terrible conquest of the world in the eighteenth year of his reign on the twenty-second day of the first month (Jdt 2:1). The eighteenth year of Nebuchadnezzar's actual reign (in Babylon) was 587 BCE, the year of Jerusalem's destruction and the beginning of the exile, the worst moment in Israel's history. The use of this date suggests that perhaps Nebuchadnezzar will indeed be successful.

But the author's setting of Nisan as the month when Nebuchadnezzar's conquest began is a symbol that Israel will not fall before this formidable enemy. The first month of the Jewish year is Nisan (March–April), the month of Passover which celebrates God's deliverance of the Israelites when they were most helpless, a pivotal moment in Israel's history. The actual month of Nebuchadnezzar's conquest of Jerusalem and the beginning of the Babylonian exile was Av (close to our August).

But if we still miss the point that God will save them no matter how great the difficulty, the author gives us one more clue. Again dates are mixed up, and yet another year is suggested. We are told that the people have just been saved by God again; they have just returned from exile (539 BCE; Jdt 4:3). So even as chapter two suggests that this is 587, their worst moment, chapter four indicates that it is really 539, the moment of their deliverance.

This mixing of dates and years and countries may seem confusing to us, but the author is not intending to give us a historical portrayal. Rather the author is telling a story that is larger than life. Israel's greatest enemies and worst defeats are all rolled into one "mega-enemy." The most dramatic examples of God's salvation throughout their history are all rolled into one "mega-rescue." Why would an author do this? This author wants to encourage the people of the second century BCE (the time when the book was likely written) to believe that God will again rescue them, that no enemy can defeat them if they cling to God. In the second century the people are threatened by King Antiochus of Syria. They fear for their lives and for the loss of their Jewish tradition. The story of Judith was written to strengthen the faith of these believers.

A Holy Widow

Judith 8:1-8

¹Now in those days Judith, daughter of Merari, son of Ox, son of Joseph, son of Oziel, son of Elkiah, son of Ananias, son of Gideon, son of Raphain, son of Ahitub, son of Elijah, son of Hilkiah, son of Eliab, son of Nathanael, son of Salamiel, son of Sarasadai, son of Simeon, son of Israel, heard of this. ²Her husband, Manasseh, of her own tribe and clan, had died at the time of the barley harvest. ³While he was supervising those who bound the sheaves in the field, he was overcome by the heat; and he collapsed on his bed and died in Bethulia, his native city. He was buried with his ancestors in the field between Dothan and Balamon. ⁴Judith was living as a widow

in her home for three years and four months. ⁵She set up a tent for herself on the roof of her house, put sackcloth about her waist, and wore widow's clothing. ⁶She fasted all the days of her widowhood, except sabbath eves and sabbaths, new moon eves and new moons, feastdays and holidays of the house of Israel. ⁷She was beautiful in appearance and very lovely to behold. Her husband, Manasseh, had left her gold and silver, male and female servants, livestock and fields, which she was maintaining. ⁸No one had a bad word to say about her, for she feared God greatly.

It might surprise readers that, in the book that bears her name, Judith does not appear until chapter eight. The first seven chapters are devoted to the accomplishments and boasting of her chief adversary, Holofernes, Nebuchadnezzar's army general. Judith, whose name means "Jewess/Woman of Judea," is introduced with a sixteen-member genealogy that goes back to Jacob (Israel). The extensive genealogy is an indication of the importance of her story in the tradition of Israel.

Judith is a widow and thus potentially marginalized in Israelite society. However, she is also wealthy. Finally, she is a holy woman. She fasts; she keeps the appropriate festivals. She is kind to everyone and God-fearing. Even the mention of her beauty is a sign that she is also holy. It is rare in the Bible that anyone is called beautiful who is not also virtuous.

Judith 8:9-27

⁹So when Judith heard of the harsh words that the people, discouraged by their lack of water, had spoken against their ruler, and of all that Uzziah had said to them in reply, swearing that he would hand over the city to the Assyrians at the end of

continue

five days, ¹⁰she sent her maid who was in charge of all her things to summon Uzziah, Chabris, and Charmis, the elders of her city. ¹¹When they came, she said to them: "Listen to me, you rulers of the people of Bethulia. What you said to the people today is not right. You pronounced this oath, made between God and yourselves, and promised to hand over the city to our enemies unless within a certain time the Lord comes to our aid. ¹²Who are you to put God to the test today, setting yourselves in the place of God in human affairs? ¹³And now it is the Lord Almighty you are putting to the test, but you will never understand anything! ¹⁴You cannot plumb the depths of the human heart or grasp the workings of the human mind; how then can you fathom God, who has made all these things, or discern his mind, or understand his plan?

"No, my brothers, do not anger the Lord our God. ¹⁵For if he does not plan to come to our aid within the five days, he has it equally within his power to protect us at such time as he pleases, or to destroy us in the sight of our enemies. ¹⁶Do not impose conditions on the plans of the Lord our God. God is not like a human being to be moved by threats, nor like a mortal to be cajoled.

¹⁷"So while we wait for the salvation that comes from him, let us call upon him to help us, and he will hear our cry if it pleases him. ¹⁸For there has not risen among us in recent generations, nor does there exist today, any tribe, or clan, or district, or city of ours that worships gods made by hands, as happened in former days. ¹⁹It was for such conduct that our ancestors were handed over to the sword and to pillage, and fell with great destruction before our enemies. ²⁰But since we acknowledge no other god but the Lord, we hope that he will not disdain us or any of our people. ²¹If we are taken, then all Judea will fall, our sanctuary will be plundered, and God will demand an account from us for their profanation. ²²For the slaughter of our kindred, for the taking of exiles from the land, and for the devastation of our inheritance, he will hold us responsible among the nations. Wherever we are enslaved, we will be a scandal and a reproach in the eyes of our masters. ²³Our servitude will not work to our advantage, but the Lord our God will turn it to disgrace.

²⁴"Therefore, my brothers, let us set an example for our kindred. Their lives depend on us, and the defense of the sanctuary, the temple, and the altar rests with us. ²⁵Besides all this, let us give thanks to the Lord our God for putting us to the test as he did our ancestors. ²⁶Recall how he dealt with Abraham, and how he tested Isaac, and all that happened to Jacob in Syrian Mesopotamia while he was tending the flocks of Laban, his mother's brother. ²⁷He has not tested us with fire, as he did them, to try their hearts, nor is he taking vengeance on us. But the Lord chastises those who are close to him in order to admonish them."

Judith has heard of the distress of her people. Holofernes has besieged the city and cut off the water supply. The people are beginning to collapse from thirst. She has also heard what the elders of the city have done. Under the leadership of Uzziah, they have given God five days to deliver them by sending help. If no help comes, they will hand over the city to the Assyrians. Judith sees the action of the elders as an act of despair. So she sends for the elders, chastises them for their failure to trust in God, reminds them of God's actions in the past, and exhorts them to have courage. Her speech reveals that she is not only prayerful but also wise. She understands the ways of God. Judith is also fearless. She does not hesitate to summon and reprove even the elders of her city. Acting as a prophet, she calls her people to radical faith in God, no matter how desperate the situation seems.

Judith 8:28-36

²⁸Then Uzziah said to her: "All that you have said you have spoken truthfully, and no one can deny your words. ²⁹For today is not the first time your wisdom has been evident, but from your earliest days all the people have recognized your

understanding, for your heart's disposition is right. ³⁰The people, however, were so thirsty that they forced us to do for them as we have promised, and to bind ourselves by an oath that we cannot break. ³¹But now, since you are a devout woman, pray for us that the Lord may send rain to fill up our cisterns. Then we will no longer be fainting from thirst."

³²Then Judith said to them: "Listen to me! I will perform a deed that will go down from generation to generation among our descendants. ³³Stand at the city gate tonight to let me pass through with my maid; and within the days you have specified before you will surrender the city to our enemies, the Lord will deliver Israel by my hand. ³⁴You must not inquire into the affair, for I will not tell you what I am doing until it has been accomplished." ³⁵Uzziah and the rulers said to her, "Go in peace, and may the Lord God go before you to take vengeance upon our enemies!" ³⁶Then they withdrew from the tent and returned to their posts.

Uzziah still cannot comprehend the truth that God's ways are not our ways. He commends Judith for her words and then asks her to pray that God will answer in the way they desire by sending rain. Judith, on the other hand, has understood that the ways of God are often surprising. She also recognizes that our cooperation with God sometimes requires us to take unconventional risks. She will not tell Uzziah her plan; she gives him only the information necessary for his part in it. He must allow her to leave the city with her maid. She assures him that the oath he swore to the people will be honored, that God will deliver them within the time that he has set.

Her Prayer

Judith 9:1-14

¹Judith fell prostrate, put ashes upon her head, and uncovered the sackcloth she was wearing. Just as the evening incense was being offered in the temple of God in Jerusalem, Judith cried loudly to the Lord: ²"Lord, God of my father Simeon, into whose hand you put a sword to take revenge upon the foreigners who had defiled a virgin by violating her, shaming her by uncovering her thighs, and dishonoring her by polluting her womb. You said, 'This shall not be done!' Yet they did it. ³Therefore you handed over their rulers to slaughter; and you handed over to bloodshed the bed in which they lay deceived, the same bed that had felt the shame of their own deceiving. You struck down the slaves together with their masters, and the masters upon their thrones. ⁴Their wives you handed over to plunder, and their daughters to captivity, and all the spoils you divided among your favored children, who burned with zeal for you and in their abhorrence of the defilement of their blood called on you for help. O God, my God, hear me also, a widow.

⁵"It is you who were the author of those events and of what preceded and followed them. The

continue

Judith *by Gabriel Ferrier (1875)*

present and the future you have also planned. Whatever you devise comes into being. ⁶The things you decide come forward and say, 'Here we are!' All your ways are in readiness, and your judgment is made with foreknowledge.

⁷"Here are the Assyrians, a vast force, priding themselves on horse and chariot, boasting of the power of their infantry, trusting in shield and spear, bow and sling. They do not know that you are the Lord who crushes wars; ⁸Lord is your name. Shatter their strength in your might, and crush their force in your wrath. For they have resolved to profane your sanctuary, to defile the tent where your glorious name resides, and to break off the horns of your altar with the sword. ⁹See their pride, and send forth your fury upon their heads. Give me, a widow, a strong hand to execute my plan. ¹⁰By the deceit of my lips, strike down slave together with ruler, and ruler together with attendant. Crush their arrogance by the hand of a female.

¹¹"Your strength is not in numbers, nor does your might depend upon the powerful. You are God of the lowly, helper of those of little account, supporter of the weak, protector of those in despair, savior of those without hope.

¹²"Please, please, God of my father, God of the heritage of Israel, Master of heaven and earth, Creator of the waters, King of all you have created, hear my prayer! ¹³Let my deceitful words wound and bruise those who have planned dire things against your covenant, your holy temple, Mount Zion, and the house your children possess. ¹⁴Make every nation and every tribe know clearly that you are God, the God of all power and might, and that there is no other who shields the people of Israel but you alone."

Judith is a woman of prayer. She knows the proper rituals for laments and prayers of petition. She dresses herself in penitential garments, sackcloth and ashes. She prostrates herself, approaching the great God from a position of lowliness and submission. She prays at an established time of prayer, the hour when the incense is

being offered in the Jerusalem temple. She has prepared for her prayer with care and attention.

Many forms of prayer are found throughout the Bible, but perhaps none as heart-wrenching as a **lament**. In a lament, an individual or community wraps together all their pain, grief, anger, and confusion in a sorrowful cry to God, begging for help or healing. The prayer of Judith is a good example of this prayer form (Jdt 9). Laments are found throughout the Bible, especially in the psalms and the prophets. Prayers of lament put us in touch with our vulnerability, provide an outlet for our emotions, keep us in dialogue with God, and offer an avenue of hope.

The content of Judith's prayer is also carefully formed. She begins in the traditional style of the lament with a cry to God (9:2). She recalls events in the past when the covenant people were victorious through God's help (9:2-4). Judith, a descendant of Simeon, recounts the story of the rape of Jacob's daughter Dinah by Shechem, which was avenged by her brothers Simeon and Levi (Gen 34; see Part One, Lesson Two). It is common in laments to tell a story of God's deliverance in the past in order to motivate God to help people in the present crisis.

Then Judith comes to the heart of her plea: "O God, my God, hear me also, a widow." Her petition is based on the contrast between her own weakness and God's power (9:5-7). It is God who is in charge of all time. It is God who is the great warrior, not these boastful Assyrians (9:7-9). This great God uses power not for glory but for love of the lowly. The strength of this great God is exercised not through the mighty but through the weak (9:11). Therefore Judith counts on God to use her, a widow, to defeat the mighty Assyrians (9:9-10).

Judith's conclusion pulls all the threads together (9:12-14). She motivates God to act with five glorious titles that express God's relationship to her, to Israel, and to all creation. In addition, she points out that the enemy is really attacking God—God's covenant, God's temple, God's people. She acknowledges that the people have no help except in God. Finally, she appeals to God's honor. Through this victory all peoples will know that Israel's God is the God of all power and might. For all these reasons God should answer her petition to use her deceitful speech and strong hand to defeat the enemy.

Judith's prayer reveals the depth of her holiness and wisdom. She has a clear understanding of God. She also understands God's care for her and for her people. She is willing and able to be an instrument of God.

Her Beauty

Judith 10:1-10

¹As soon as Judith had ceased her prayer to the God of Israel and finished all these words, ²she rose from the ground. She called her maid and they went down into the house, which she used only on sabbaths and feast days. ³She took off the sackcloth she had on, laid aside the garments of her widowhood, washed her body with water, and anointed herself with rich ointment. She arranged her hair, put on a diadem, and dressed in the festive attire she had worn while her husband, Manasseh, was living. ⁴She chose sandals for her feet, and put on her anklets, bracelets, rings, earrings, and all her other jewelry. Thus she made herself very beautiful, to entice the eyes of all the men who should see her.

⁵She gave her maid a skin of wine and a jug of oil. She filled a bag with roasted grain, dried fig cakes, and pure bread. She wrapped all her dishes and gave them to the maid to carry.

⁶Then they went out to the gate of the city of Bethulia and found Uzziah and the elders of the city, Chabris and Charmis, standing there. ⁷When they saw Judith transformed in looks and differently dressed, they were very much astounded at her beauty and said to her, ⁸"May the God of our ancestors grant you favor and make your design successful, for the glory of the Israelites and the exaltation of Jerusalem." ⁹Judith bowed down to God.

Then she said to them, "Order the gate of the city opened for me, that I may go to accomplish the matters we discussed." So they ordered the young men to open the gate for her, as she had requested, ¹⁰and they did so. Then Judith and her maidservant went out. The men of the city kept her in view as she went down the mountain and crossed the valley; then they lost sight of her.

Judith turns to other necessities to carry out her plan. She will use the weapon of beauty and charm to deliver God's people from the enemy. She dresses carefully, "to entice the eyes of all the men who should see her." Her preparations are successful. The men of her town are astounded at her beauty. She also enlists the help of her maid and prepares food so that they will not break the Jewish dietary laws by

Judith and her maid. Sandro Botticelli (1470)

eating the food of the enemy. Thus armed, she sets out for the enemy camp.

Judith is an example to her fearful people of courage and trust in God. She and her maid go out to the enemy camp, depending completely on the power of God. Just as Israel had no defense but God at the Red Sea, so Judith has nothing but God to protect her in the Assyrian camp. She has taken to heart the words of Psalm 20:8-9: "Some rely on chariots, others on horses, / but we on the name of the LORD our God. / They collapse and fall, / but we stand strong and firm."

Her Wit

Judith 10:11-19

[11]As Judith and her maid walked directly across the valley, they encountered the Assyrian patrol. [12]The men took her in custody and asked her, "To what people do you belong? Where do you come from, and where are you going?" She replied: "I am a daughter of the Hebrews, and I

More Women of the Old Testament

The Shunammite Woman

The Shunammite woman is a notable figure in biblical narratives about the prophet Elisha in 2 Kings (4:8-37; 8:1-6). In terms of location in the Bible, she could be featured in Lesson One (Women of Israel's Monarchy), but in terms of her character and story, she is best featured in this lesson with its focus on women of courage and strength.

The Shunammite woman is first mentioned when Elisha passes through the city of Shunem. She is called a "woman of influence" (*'ishah gedolah*). This Hebrew term means "great woman" and could refer to her status in society, her influence, and/or her financial wealth. The woman observes Elisha, a man of God, and offers him hospitality. She insists that she and her husband provide Elisha room and board when he comes to their town.

The Shunammite woman recognizes prophetic power and shows authority, initiative, and control over her household in her decision-making and advocacy. Elisha acknowledges her significance and says that she will be blessed with a son. The woman conceives and bears a child who later becomes ill and dies. Many biblical narratives feature women in passive roles, but 2 Kings depicts the Shunammite woman as a woman of strength who takes charge to help her son. She finds Elisha at Mount Carmel and demands that he return to save her son, which he does. She maintains composure and control, managing the crisis, giving instructions to servants, and relaying information to her husband.

In the second narrative, Elisha tells the woman that a famine is forthcoming. The woman relocates her family for the length of the famine and returns to find that her land has apparently been seized. The woman (not her husband, which would have been customary) appeals to the king for her house and land, actions that suggest her ownership. As a result of her testimony, her land is restored, and she is granted all the produce of the field from the time she was gone.

The Shunammite woman is a great example of strength and courage, demonstrating skillful and successful advocacy for herself and her family in difficult periods of loss.

—*Jaime L. Waters*

am fleeing from them, because they are about to be delivered up to you as prey. ¹³I have come to see Holofernes, the ranking general of your forces, to give him a trustworthy report; in his presence I will show him the way by which he can ascend and take possession of the whole hill country without a single one of his men suffering injury or loss of life."

¹⁴When the men heard her words and gazed upon her face, which appeared marvelously beautiful to them, they said to her, ¹⁵"By hastening down to see our master, you have saved your life. Now go to his tent; some of us will accompany you to hand you over to him. ¹⁶When you stand before him, have no fear in your heart; give him the report you have given us, and he will treat you well." ¹⁷So they selected a hundred of their men as an escort for her and her maid, and these conducted them to the tent of Holofernes.

¹⁸As the news of her arrival spread among the tents, a crowd gathered in the camp. They came and stood around her as she waited outside the tent of Holofernes, while he was being informed about her. ¹⁹They marveled at her beauty, regarding the Israelites with wonder because of her, and they said to one another, "Who can despise this people who have such women among them? It is not good to leave one of their men alive, for if any were to be spared they could beguile the whole earth."

It is not only the Israelite men who are astounded at Judith's beauty. The men of the Assyrian camp are equally dazed. For the sake of her beauty they admire her whole people. Her beauty has won her acceptance in the enemy camp.

Judith has also asked for a second weapon, deceitful speech. She begins weaving her web of deceit by hinting that Holofernes will be successful. She can indeed show him a route by which he could conquer. He will not be able to do so, however, because the successful outcome of her plan will leave him dead.

Judith 10:20–11:23

²⁰Then the guards of Holofernes and all his attendants came out and ushered her into the tent. ²¹Holofernes was reclining on his bed under a canopy woven of purple, gold, emeralds, and other precious stones. ²²When they announced her to him, he came out to the front part of the tent, preceded by silver lamps. ²³When Judith came before Holofernes and his attendants, they all marveled at the beauty of her face. She fell prostrate and paid homage to him, but his servants raised her up.

¹¹:¹Then Holofernes said to her: "Take courage, woman! Have no fear in your heart! I have never harmed anyone who chose to serve Nebuchadnezzar, king of all the earth. ²As for your people who live in the hill country, I would never have raised my spear against them, had they not insulted me. They have brought this upon themselves. ³But now tell me why you have fled from them and come to us? In any case, you have come to safety. Take courage! Your life is spared tonight and for the future. ⁴No one at all will harm you. Rather, you will be well treated, as are the servants of my lord, King Nebuchadnezzar."

⁵Judith answered him: "Listen to the words of your servant, and let your maidservant speak in your presence! I will say nothing false to my lord this night. ⁶If you follow the words of your maidservant, God will successfully perform a deed through you, and my lord will not fail to achieve his designs. ⁷I swear by the life of Nebuchadnezzar, king of all the earth, and by the power of him who has sent you to guide all living things, that not only do human beings serve him through you; but even the wild animals, and the cattle, and the birds of the air, because of your strength, will live for Nebuchadnezzar and his whole house. ⁸Indeed, we have heard of your wisdom and cleverness. The whole earth is aware that you above all others in the kingdom are able, rich in experience, and distinguished in military strategy.

⁹"As for Achior's speech in your council, we have heard it. When the men of Bethulia rescued him,

continue

he told them all he had said to you. ¹⁰So then, my lord and master, do not disregard his word, but bear it in mind, for it is true. Indeed our people are not punished, nor does the sword prevail against them, except when they sin against their God. ¹¹But now their sin has caught up with them, by which they will bring the wrath of their God upon them when they do wrong; so that my lord will not be repulsed and fail, but death will overtake them. ¹²Because their food has given out and all their water is running low, they have decided to kill their animals, and are determined to consume all the things which God in his laws has forbidden them to eat. ¹³They have decided that they would use the first fruits of grain and the tithes of wine and oil, which they had consecrated and reserved for the priests who minister in the presence of our God in Jerusalem—things which the people should not so much as touch with their hands. ¹⁴They have sent messengers to Jerusalem to bring back permission from the senate, for even there people have done these things. ¹⁵On the very day when the response reaches them and they act upon it, they will be handed over to you for destruction.

¹⁶"As soon as I, your servant, learned all this, I fled from them. God has sent me to perform with you such deeds as will astonish people throughout the whole earth who hear of them. ¹⁷Your servant is, indeed, a God-fearing woman, serving the God of heaven night and day. Now I will remain with you, my lord; but each night your servant will go out into the valley and pray to God. He will tell me when they have committed their offenses. ¹⁸Then I will come and let you know, so that you may march out with all your forces, and not one of them will be able to withstand you. ¹⁹I will lead you through the heart of Judea until you come to Jerusalem, and there in its center I will set up your throne. You will drive them like sheep that have no shepherd, and not even a dog will growl at you. This was told to me in advance and announced to me, and I have been sent to tell you."

²⁰Her words pleased Holofernes and all his attendants. They marveled at her wisdom and exclaimed, ²¹"No other woman from one end of the earth to the other looks so beautiful and speaks so wiscly!" ²²Then Holofernes said to her: "God

has done well in sending you ahead of your people, to bring victory to our hands, and destruction to those who have despised my lord. ²³You are not only beautiful in appearance, but you are also eloquent. If you do as you have said, your God will be my God; you will live in the palace of King Nebuchadnezzar and be renowned throughout the whole earth."

The first two weapons in Judith's arsenal, beauty and wit, are wonderfully effective. Like the rest of the Assyrian camp, Holofernes marvels at her beauty. Her words, a mixture of truth and deceit, are even more powerful. The general is so vain that he interprets everything she says to his own benefit. When she says that she will tell no lie to her lord and that her lord will not fail in any of his undertakings, Holofernes assumes that she is speaking of him. But it is her Lord God who will not fail. She tells Holofernes that if he follows her words, God will give him complete success. It is true that if he follows her words and lives according to God's law, he will be successful. But she knows he will not do this.

Judith also reports that Achior's testimony is reliable: Israel will only be defeated if they are sinful. The book of Judith shares similarities with the book of Judges. When the people are faithful, they are also victorious; when they sin, they are defeated. Judith has already declared to the elders that she expects victory because the people have not turned away from the Lord to other gods (8:17-20). The reader can thus assume that the people have been faithful, even though Judith suggests to Holofernes that they have broken the dietary laws because they have no other food (11:12-13). There are indications that they in truth still have food that they are permitted to eat, since Judith was able to provide herself with enough proper food for her sojourn in the enemy camp.

Judith's suggestion to Holofernes that the people have been unfaithful can be assumed to be part of her deceit. She warns Holofernes that God's people are not punished unless they sin ("our people are not punished, nor does the sword prevail against them, except when they sin against their God"). But then she cunningly suggests that "their sin has caught up with them" and that Holofernes will be able to conquer them. He hears what he wants to hear. He misses the possibility that they may be faithful to God and thus protected.

Finally Judith says to him, "God has sent me to perform with you such deeds as will astonish people throughout the whole earth who hear of them." She warns him further that she is God-fearing and prayerful. She tells him clearly where the source of her power lies. She is faithful, therefore God will grant her victory. Still Holofernes does not understand. Unaware that he speaks his own disaster, he concludes their meeting: "God has done well in sending you ahead of your people." Indeed!

Judith 12:1-9

¹Then he ordered them to lead her into the room where his silver dinnerware was kept, and ordered them to set a table for her with his own delicacies to eat and his own wine to drink. ²But Judith said, "I cannot eat any of them, because it would be a scandal. Besides, I will have enough with the things I brought with me." ³Holofernes asked her, "But if your provisions give out, where can we get more of the same to provide for you? None of your people are with us." ⁴Judith answered him, "As surely as you live, my lord, your servant will not use up her supplies before the Lord accomplishes by my hand what he has determined."

⁵Then the attendants of Holofernes led her to her tent, where she slept until the middle of the night. Toward the early morning watch, she rose ⁶and sent this message to Holofernes, "Give orders, my lord, to let your servant go out for prayer." ⁷So Holofernes ordered his guards not to hinder her. Thus she stayed in the camp three days. Each night she went out to the valley of Bethulia, where she bathed herself at the spring

of the camp. ⁸After bathing, she prayed to the Lord, the God of Israel, to direct her way for the triumph of her people. ⁹Then she returned purified to the tent and remained there until her food was brought to her toward evening.

Judith continues to be faithful to her religious practices and to deceive Holofernes even when she tells the truth. She observes the Jewish dietary regulations scrupulously; she speaks truly when she tells the general that she will not run out of food before God works through her to accomplish the divine will. She also leaves the camp each evening to bathe and to pray. This practice not only demonstrates her fidelity, it will also provide her escape. Her daily schedule creates a way she can leave the camp without arousing the suspicion of the guards. Judith's wit continues to be a formidable weapon.

Her Strong Hand

Judith 12:10–13:3

¹⁰On the fourth day Holofernes gave a banquet for his servants alone, to which he did not invite any of the officers. ¹¹And he said to Bagoas, the eunuch in charge of his personal affairs, "Go and persuade the Hebrew woman in your care to come and to eat and drink with us. ¹²It would bring shame on us to be with such a woman without enjoying her. If we do not seduce her, she will laugh at us."

¹³So Bagoas left the presence of Holofernes, and came to Judith and said, "So lovely a maidservant should not be reluctant to come to my lord to be honored by him, to enjoy drinking wine with us, and to act today like one of the Assyrian women who serve in the palace of Nebuchadnezzar." ¹⁴Judith replied, "Who am I to refuse my lord?

continue

Whatever is pleasing to him I will promptly do. This will be a joy for me until the day of my death."

¹⁵So she proceeded to put on her festive garments and all her finery. Meanwhile her servant went ahead and spread out on the ground opposite Holofernes the fleece Bagoas had furnished for her daily use in reclining while eating. ¹⁶Then Judith came in and reclined. The heart of Holofernes was in rapture over her and his passion was aroused. He was burning with the desire to possess her, for he had been biding his time to seduce her from the day he saw her. ¹⁷Holofernes said to her, "Drink and be happy with us!" ¹⁸Judith replied, "I will gladly drink, my lord, for today is the greatest day of my whole life." ¹⁹She then took the things her servant had prepared and ate and drank in his presence. ²⁰Holofernes, charmed by her, drank a great quantity of wine, more than he had ever drunk on any day since he was born.

¹³:¹When it grew late, his servants quickly withdrew. Bagoas closed the tent from the outside and dismissed the attendants from their master's presence. They went off to their beds, for they were all tired because the banquet had lasted so long. ²Judith was left alone in the tent with Holofernes, who lay sprawled on his bed, for he was drunk with wine. ³Judith had ordered her maidservant to stand outside the bedchamber and to wait, as on the other days, for her to come out; she had said she would be going out for her prayer. She had also said this same thing to Bagoas.

The Assyrians have fatally misunderstood Judith. They have seen only her beauty and missed her wisdom. Holofernes sends his servant to bring Judith to his table and his bed, declaring that it would be a disgrace not to enjoy and take possession of such beauty. He has been waiting for a moment to seduce her. Holofernes is so intoxicated by Judith's beauty that he becomes totally drunk on wine. It is the familiar story of lust and sexual conquest in which the woman becomes simply an object to satisfy the man's desire (e.g., Amnon for Tamar). In this story, however, it is the man

himself who will be destroyed by his action. Holofernes' focus on Judith's beauty and disregard of her wit will be his undoing.

Judith, on the other hand, continues to use the weapons of both beauty and wisdom. She adorns herself for the encounter. She makes true statements that would warn Holofernes if he were not blinded by arrogance. She declares that pleasing her "lord" (God) is a lasting joy to her; Holofernes assumes that he is her lord. She exclaims that this is the happiest day of her life; Holofernes does not realize that it is his anticipated death that gives her such delight. He has been lured into totally underestimating his enemy.

Judith 13:4-10

⁴When all had departed, and no one, small or great, was left in the bedchamber, Judith stood by Holofernes' bed and prayed silently, "O Lord, God of all might, in this hour look graciously on the work of my hands for the exaltation of Jerusalem. ⁵Now is the time for aiding your heritage and for carrying out my design to shatter the enemies who have risen against us." ⁶She went to the bedpost near the head of Holofernes, and taking his sword from it, ⁷she drew close to the bed, grasped the hair of his head, and said, "Strengthen me this day, Lord, God of Israel!" ⁸Then with all her might she struck his neck twice and cut off his head. ⁹She rolled his body off the bed and took the canopy from its posts. Soon afterward, she came out and handed over the head of Holofernes to her maid, ¹⁰who put it into her food bag. Then the two went out together for prayer as they were accustomed to do.

Finally the critical moment arrives. Holofernes is drunk on his bed. Everyone else has left. The time has come for the use of Judith's third weapon, her strong hand. She prepares herself with prayer, acknowledging again her conviction that it is through God's power that she acts. Strengthened by God, Judith beheads Holofernes. She uses his own sword,

An unnamed and seemingly insignificant character, **Judith's maid** appears twice in the story of Judith. Her first appearance occurs just after Judith sheds her sackcloth and readies herself for victory over Israel's enemy. Her maid is there to carry Judith's provisions. Readers picture a steady and trusted companion, one who is ready to fulfill her duty, a woman of physical strength and a willing spirit.

The maid's second appearance follows the gruesome scene when Judith has killed Holofernes, decapitated him, and recovered his head as evidence of Israel's victory. Once again, her maid is there to carry whatever her mistress has given her. It is both ghastly and humorous to think of these two women calmly packing away the evidence and returning to camp.

Judith is sometimes hailed as a kind of female Moses, a liberator who delivers Israel from its enemies. Perhaps Judith's maid is like Aaron and Miriam, an essential partner in a new story of liberation.

the weapon that has killed and subjugated so many people. She has accomplished what she set out to do: she has killed the enemy of her people. Through her, God has saved Israel.

When Judith emerges from Holofernes' tent, she hands Holofernes' head to her maid who puts it into the food pouch. The maid is a valued partner in Judith's courageous enterprise. It was the maid who first summoned the elders to Judith's house. The maid helps with her initial preparations. The maid is her companion in the enemy camp and goes out with her to pray each evening. The maid prepares her for the final encounter with Holofernes and then stands guard. Now this brave woman accepts the severed head of the enemy from her mistress and calmly stows it away for the return journey to the camp. The maid, though often invisible and ignored, is essential to Judith's success.

Blessed Among Women

Judith 13:10-20

They passed through the camp, and skirting that valley, went up the mountain to Bethulia, and approached its gates. [11]From a distance,

Judith shouted to the guards at the gates: "Open! Open the gate! God, our God, is with us. Once more he has shown his strength in Israel and his power against the enemy, as he has today!"

[12]When the citizens heard her voice, they hurried down to their city gate and summoned the elders of the city. [13]All the people, from the least to the greatest, hurriedly assembled, for her return seemed unbelievable. They opened the gate and welcomed the two women. They made a fire for light and gathered around the two. [14]Judith urged them with a loud voice: "Praise God, give praise! Praise God, who has not withdrawn his mercy from the house of Israel, but has shattered our enemies by my hand this very night!" [15]Then she took the head out of the bag, showed it to them, and said: "Here is the head of Holofernes, the ranking general of the Assyrian forces, and here is the canopy under which he lay in his drunkenness. The Lord struck him down by the hand of a female! [16]Yet I swear by the Lord, who has protected me in the way I have walked, that it was my face that seduced Holofernes to his ruin, and that he did not defile me with sin or shame."

[17]All the people were greatly astonished. They bowed down and worshiped God, saying with one accord, "Blessed are you, our God, who today have humiliated the enemies of your people." [18]Then

continue

Uzziah said to her, "Blessed are you, daughter, by the Most High God, above all the women on earth; and blessed be the Lord God, the creator of heaven and earth, who guided your blow at the head of the leader of our enemies. ¹⁹Your deed of hope will never be forgotten by those who recall the might of God. ²⁰May God make this redound to your everlasting honor, rewarding you with blessings, because you risked your life when our people were being oppressed, and you averted our disaster, walking in the straight path before our God." And all the people answered, "Amen! Amen!"

When the two women arrive at the gate of Bethulia, the townspeople can hardly believe that they have been delivered from the enemy. Even as she demonstrates the truth of Holofernes' death, she urges the people to remember their true Deliverer: "Praise God!" The people respond to her exhortation and pray in thanksgiving and praise. She reminds them that God brings victory to the righteous; she assures them that she has not sinned with

Judith shows the people the head of Holofernes. Gustave Dore (1870)

Holofernes (13:16). Uzziah, who thought deliverance could only come in the form of rain, adds praise of Judith to his praise of God. He honors her for risking her life and acting as God's instrument of redemption. He calls her blessed "above all the women on earth," echoing Deborah's praise of Jael, who also killed an enemy general (Judg 5:24). The people's agreement sounds in their "Amen!"

The violence in Judith's action and the people's delight in her success may horrify and offend modern readers of the story. It is helpful to remember the deeper significance the author is trying to convey: no matter how helpless God's people are in the face of their enemies, God will deliver them. Christians see God's greatest deliverance in the death and resurrection of Jesus, an event in which horrible violence is overcome by absolute faith and undying love.

The Victory

Judith 14:1-10

¹Then Judith said to them: "Listen to me, my brothers and sisters. Take this head and hang it on the parapet of your wall. ²At daybreak, when the sun rises on the earth, each of you seize your weapons, and let all the able-bodied men rush out of the city under command of a captain, as if about to go down into the valley against the Assyrian patrol, but without going down. ³The Assyrians will seize their weapons and hurry to their camp to awaken the generals of the army. When they run to the tent of Holofernes and do not find him, panic will seize them, and they will flee before you. ⁴Then you and all the other inhabitants of the whole territory of Israel will pursue them and strike them down in their tracks. ⁵But before doing this, summon for me Achior the Ammonite, that he may see and recognize the one who despised the house of Israel and sent him here to meet his death."

⁶So they called Achior from the house of Uzziah. When he came and saw the head of Holofernes in

the hand of one of the men in the assembly of the people, he collapsed in a faint. ⁷Then, after they lifted him up, he threw himself at the feet of Judith in homage, saying: "Blessed are you in every tent of Judah! In every nation, all who hear your name will be struck with terror. ⁸But now, tell me all that you did during these days." So Judith told him, in the midst of the people, all that she had done, from the day she left until the time she began speaking to them. ⁹When she had finished her account, the people cheered loudly, so that the city resounded with shouts of joy. ¹⁰Now Achior, seeing all that the God of Israel had done, believed firmly in God. He circumcised the flesh of his foreskin and he has been united with the house of Israel to the present day.

The victory is not yet complete; the Assyrian army is still encamped outside the city. Judith takes on the role of general and describes the plan of attack. She also sends for Achior, the leader of Israel's neighbor and sometimes opponent, the Ammonites. Achior had been summoned by Holofernes when the Assyrians arrived at Bethulia to give him information about the Israelites. Achior had reported that the Israelites are victorious when they are faithful to God but can be defeated when they are sinful (Jdt 5:5-24). Judith now needs him to witness to her fellow townspeople that the man she has beheaded is truly Holofernes. When Achior recognizes the head, he faints; then he joins in the praise of Judith. Her story leads him to faith in Israel's God. Achior is a dramatic contrast to Judith. The military man faints; the woman empowered by God overcomes the enemy.

Judith 14:11–15:3

¹¹At daybreak they hung the head of Holofernes on the wall. Then all the Israelite men took up their weapons and went out by groups to the mountain passes. ¹²When the Assyrians saw them, they notified their commanders, who, in turn, went to their generals, their division leaders, and all their other leaders. ¹³They came to the tent of Holofernes and said to the one in charge of all his things, "Awaken our lord, for the slaves have dared come down against us in battle, to their utter destruction." ¹⁴So Bagoas went in and knocked at the entry of the tent, presuming that Holofernes was sleeping with Judith. ¹⁵When no one answered, he parted the curtains, entered the bedchamber, and found him thrown on the floor dead, with his head gone! ¹⁶He cried out loudly, weeping, groaning, and howling, and tore his garments. ¹⁷Then he entered the tent where Judith had her quarters; and, not finding her, he rushed out to the troops and cried: ¹⁸"The slaves have duped us! One Hebrew woman has brought shame on the house of King Nebuchadnezzar. Look! Holofernes on the ground—without a head!"

¹⁹When the leaders of the Assyrian forces heard these words, they tore their tunics and were overcome with great distress. Their loud cries and shouts were heard throughout the camp.

¹⁵:¹On hearing what had happened, those still in their tents were horrified. ²Overcome with fear and dread, no one kept ranks any longer. They scattered in all directions, and fled along every path, both through the valley and in the hill country. ³Those who were stationed in the hill country around Bethulia also took to flight. Then the Israelites, every warrior among them, came charging down upon them.

The Assyrians realize too late that Judith is more than beauty. Holofernes' servant, still blindly assuming that his master is sleeping, discovers instead the headless corpse. A search reveals that Judith has escaped. Only then does he recognize the truth of Judith's power: "One Hebrew woman has brought shame on the house of King Nebuchadnezzar." His announcement is the final blow for the Assyrian army, and they flee in disorder. A Hebrew woman has won the victory for God.

Judith 15:4-13

⁴Uzziah sent messengers to Betomasthaim, to Choba and Kona, and to the whole territory of Israel to report what had happened and to urge them all to attack the enemy and destroy them. ⁵On hearing this, all the Israelites, with one accord, attacked them and cut them down as far as Choba. Even those from Jerusalem and the rest of the hill country took part in this, for they too had been notified of the happenings in the camp of their enemy. The Gileadites and the Galileans struck the enemy's flanks with great slaughter, even beyond Damascus and its borders. ⁶The remaining people of Bethulia swept down on the camp of the Assyrians, plundered it, and acquired great riches. ⁷The Israelites, when they returned from the slaughter, took possession of what was left. Even the towns and villages in the hill country and on the plain got an enormous quantity of spoils, for there was a tremendous amount of it.

⁸Then the high priest Joakim and the senate of the Israelites who lived in Jerusalem came to see for themselves the good things that the Lord had done for Israel, and to meet and congratulate Judith. ⁹When they came to her, all with one accord blessed her, saying:

"You are the glory of Jerusalem!
    You are the great pride of Israel!
    You are the great boast of our nation!
¹⁰By your own hand you have done all this.
    You have done good things for Israel,
    and God is pleased with them.
May the Almighty Lord bless you forever!"
And all the people said, "Amen!"

¹¹For thirty days all the people plundered the camp, giving Judith the tent of Holofernes, with all his silver, his beds, his dishes, and all his furniture. She took them and loaded her mule, hitched her carts, and loaded these things on them. ¹²All the women of Israel gathered to see her, and they blessed her and performed a dance in her honor. She took branches in her hands and distributed them to the women around her, ¹³and

she and the other women crowned themselves with olive leaves. Then, at the head of all the people, she led the women in the dance, while the men of Israel followed, bearing their weapons, wearing garlands and singing songs of praise.

The Israelite army completes the defeat of the Assyrians and returns to Bethulia loaded with goods. For a month all the people of Israel celebrate the victory. They plunder the camp and give Judith what belonged to Holofernes. The women bless Judith and dance in her honor; the men, dressed in their armor and following behind, sing hymns. The Jerusalem priests and elders also bless her.

The Victory Song

Judith 15:14–16:17

¹⁴Judith led all Israel in this song of thanksgiving, and the people loudly sang this hymn of praise:
¹⁶:¹And Judith sang:
"Strike up a song to my God with
        tambourines,
    sing to the Lord with cymbals;
Improvise for him a new song,
    exalt and acclaim his name.
²For the Lord is a God who crushes wars;
    he sets his encampment among his people;
    he delivered me from the hands of my
        pursuers.
³"The Assyrian came from the mountains of
        the north,
    with myriads of his forces he came;
Their numbers blocked the wadies,
    their cavalry covered the hills.
⁴He threatened to burn my territory,
    put my youths to the sword,

Dash my infants to the ground,
seize my children as plunder.
And carry off my virgins as spoil.
⁵"But the Lord Almighty thwarted them,
by the hand of a female!
⁶Not by youths was their champion struck
down,
nor did Titans bring him low,
nor did tall giants attack him;
But Judith, the daughter of Merari,
by the beauty of her face brought him down.
⁷She took off her widow's garb
to raise up the afflicted in Israel.
She anointed her face with fragrant oil;
⁸fixed her hair with a diadem,
and put on a linen robe to beguile him.
⁹Her sandals ravished his eyes,
her beauty captivated his mind,
the sword cut through his neck!
¹⁰"The Persians trembled at her boldness,
the Medes were daunted at her daring.
¹¹When my lowly ones shouted,
and my weak ones cried out,
The enemy was terrified,
screamed and took to flight.
¹²Sons of maidservants pierced them through;
wounded them like deserters' children.
They perished before the ranks of my
Lord.
¹³"I will sing a new song to my God.
O Lord, great are you and glorious,
marvelous in power and unsurpassable.
¹⁴Let your every creature serve you;
for you spoke, and they were made.
You sent forth your spirit, and it created them;
no one can resist your voice.
¹⁵For the mountains to their bases
are tossed with the waters;
the rocks, like wax, melt before your
glance.
"But to those who fear you,
you will show mercy.
¹⁶Though the sweet fragrance of every
sacrifice is a trifle,

and the fat of all burnt offerings but little
in your sight,
one who fears the Lord is forever great.
¹⁷"Woe to the nations that rise against my
people!
the Lord Almighty will requite them;
in the day of judgment he will punish them:
He will send fire and worms into their flesh,
and they will weep and suffer forever."

Judith's story is framed by prayer (see Jdt 9). Throughout her daring exploit and the congratulations that follow, she continues to declare that she did not act through her own power but through the power of God. She consistently turns her people's praise of her to praise of God.

After the victory is won, Judith takes up the role of women in the Holy War tradition. Miriam led the women in song and dance after their escape from Egypt (Exod 15:20-21). Deborah led the song of praise after the defeat of Sisera (Judg 5:1). Jephthah's daughter, whose story ends in tragedy, comes out to celebrate her father's victory over the Ammonites with music and dancing (Judg 11:34). Judith leads the song of thanksgiving in praise of God who has delivered the people from the Assyrians.

Judith's song begins as a hymn. There is a call to praise God (16:1), and the reasons for praise are given (16:2). The story of the victory is then told as an extended reason for praise (16:3-12). The final section stretches the form as God is addressed directly (16:13-15), not common in hymns. The song ends with praise of God-fearers and a woe upon their enemies (16:16-17). Original material is found in the song's description of victory (16:3-12); the remaining verses echo material from the books of Judges, Psalms, and Isaiah. In verses 3-12, Judith's beauty is highlighted as the weapon that disabled the enemy. The first and last sections (16:1-2, 13-17) set Judith's action in the context of God's continued protection of the people.

Respected Widow

Judith 16:18-25

¹⁸When they arrived at Jerusalem, they worshiped God. As soon as the people were purified, they offered their burnt offerings, voluntary offerings, and donations. ¹⁹Judith dedicated to God all the things of Holofernes that the people had given her, putting under the ban the canopy that she herself had taken from his bedchamber. ²⁰For three months the people continued their celebration in Jerusalem before the sanctuary, and Judith remained with them.

²¹When those days were over, all of them returned to their inheritance. Judith went back to Bethulia and remained on her estate. For the rest of her life she was renowned throughout the land. ²²Many wished to marry her, but she gave herself to no man all the days of her life from the time her husband, Manasseh, died and was gathered to his people. ²³Her fame continued to increase, and she lived in the house of her husband, reaching the advanced age of one hundred and five. She set her maid free. And when she died in Bethulia, they buried her in the cave of her husband, Manasseh; ²⁴and the house of Israel mourned her for seven days. Before she died, she distributed her property to the relatives of her husband, Manasseh, and to her own relatives.

²⁵During the lifetime of Judith and for a long time after her death, no one ever again spread terror among the Israelites.

At the conclusion of the story we find Judith again at home, an honored and respected widow. She arranges all her affairs with wisdom. She donates the spoil from Holofernes to the sanctuary. She distributes her wealth to her relatives and those of her husband. She gives the faithful maid her freedom.

Judith's long life is a sign of God's blessing upon her and upon the people. As long as she lives, and even afterwards, they have peace. The book's final verse ranks Judith with the judges, those men and women who saved Israel from their enemies during the pioneer period (cf. Judg 3:11, 30; 5:31; 8:28). She is the glory of Jerusalem, the joy of Israel, the splendid boast of her people.

 Several verses of praise for Judith are used by the church on **feasts of Mary**. Uzziah's praise (13:18-20) is one of the responsorial psalms listed in the Common of the Blessed Virgin. The people's praise (15:9-10) is also used in the Common of the Blessed Virgin, as well as an antiphon for both Morning and Evening Prayer on the Solemnity of the Immaculate Conception. Like Judith, Mary is praised as the glory of Jerusalem, blessed among women, who was guided by God to strike "at the head of the leader of our enemies" (13:18).

SUSANNA

The Greek tradition of the book of Daniel is longer than the Hebrew tradition. The longer manuscript, which includes the stories of Susanna (Dan 13) and Bel and the Dragon (Dan 14), is followed in Catholic and Orthodox Bibles but not Jewish or Protestant Bibles, which follow the Hebrew tradition. The Greek additions to Daniel complement and build on themes found in the book.

A Faithful Wife

Daniel 13:1-4

¹In Babylon there lived a man named Joakim, ²who married a very beautiful and God-fearing woman, Susanna, the daughter of Hilkiah; ³her parents were righteous and had trained their daughter according to the law of Moses. ⁴Joakim was very rich and he had a garden near his house. The Jews had recourse to him often because he was the most respected of them all.

The story begins by introducing the central character, Susanna, and her husband Joakim. Susanna is beautiful, God-fearing, and well-trained in the law. She is a model Jewish woman. Her husband Joakim is rich and respected. The couple are living in exile, and thus become an example to Jews living outside of Israel of how a faithful life can be lived in any place.

Daniel 13:5-14

[5]That year, two elders of the people were appointed judges, of whom the Lord said, "Lawlessness has come out of Babylon, that is, from the elders who were to govern the people as judges." [6]These men, to whom all brought their cases, frequented the house of Joakim. [7]When the people left at noon, Susanna used to enter her husband's garden for a walk. [8]When the elders saw her enter every day for her walk, they began to lust for her. [9]They perverted their thinking; they would not allow their eyes to look to heaven, and did not keep in mind just judgments. [10]Though both were enamored of her, they did not tell each other their trouble, [11]for they were ashamed to reveal their lustful desire to have her. [12]Day by day they watched eagerly for her. [13]One day they said to each other, "Let us be off for home, it is time for the noon meal." So they went their separate ways. [14]But both turned back and arrived at the same spot. When they asked each other the reason, they admitted their lust, and then they agreed to look for an occasion when they could find her alone.

The peaceful scene does not last long. Two official representatives of the religious tradition, expected to be both wise and holy, are neither. These two judges lust after Susanna. Not only that, they nourish their lust and avoid prayer lest the lust be diminished. Their consciences cannot be completely suppressed, however, and so each is ashamed to tell the other of his desire. But one day they catch each other looking for Susanna and reveal their evil intentions. Now they conspire together to find Susanna alone, and Susanna is not aware of their scheming.

Virtuous and Courageous

Daniel 13:15-27

[15]One day, while they were waiting for the right moment, she entered as usual, with two maids only, wanting to bathe in the garden, for the weather was warm. [16]Nobody else was there except the two elders, who had hidden themselves and were watching her. [17]"Bring me oil and soap," she said to the maids, "and shut the garden gates while I bathe." [18]They did as she said; they shut the garden gates and left by the side gate to fetch what she had ordered, unaware that the elders were hidden inside.

[19]As soon as the maids had left, the two old men got up and ran to her. [20]"Look," they said, "the garden doors are shut, no one can see us, and we want you. So give in to our desire, and lie with us. [21]If you refuse, we will testify against you that a young man was here with you and that is why you sent your maids away."

[22]"I am completely trapped," Susanna groaned. "If I yield, it will be my death; if I refuse, I cannot escape your power. [23]Yet it is better for me not to do it and to fall into your power than to sin before the Lord." [24]Then Susanna screamed, and the two old men also shouted at her, [25]as one of them ran to open the garden gates. [26]When the people in the house heard the cries from the garden, they rushed in by the side gate to see what had happened to her. [27]At the accusations of the old men, the servants felt very much ashamed, for never had any such thing been said about Susanna.

The two old men find their opportunity. Susanna is alone in the garden bathing. They approach her, expecting certain conquest. If Susanna will not submit to their lust, they will testify to her adultery with another man. In Israelite law the testimony of two witnesses was sufficient to convict. If Susanna resists she could be convicted of adultery and executed by stoning (Lev 20:10; Deut 22:22-24).

The two elders, however, have underestimated Susanna's strength, her virtue. She entrusts her case to God and sounds the alarm. The old men stand by their word and accuse her of adultery. Their accusation is apparently believed, and it seems Susanna faces certain execution.

Susanna Accused

Daniel 13:28-43

²⁸When the people came to her husband Joakim the next day, the two wicked old men also came, full of lawless intent to put Susanna to death. ²⁹Before the people they ordered: "Send for Susanna, the daughter of Hilkiah, the wife of Joakim." When she was sent for, ³⁰she came with her parents, children and all her relatives. ³¹Susanna, very delicate and beautiful, ³²was veiled; but those transgressors of the law ordered that she be exposed so as to sate themselves with her beauty. ³³All her companions and the onlookers were weeping.

³⁴In the midst of the people the two old men rose up and laid their hands on her head. ³⁵As she wept she looked up to heaven, for she trusted in the Lord wholeheartedly. ³⁶The old men said, "As we were walking in the garden alone, this woman entered with two servant girls, shut the garden gates and sent the servant girls away. ³⁷A young man, who was hidden there, came and lay with her. ³⁸When we, in a corner of the garden, saw this lawlessness, we ran toward them. ³⁹We saw them lying together, but the man we could not hold, because he was stronger than we; he opened the gates and ran off. ⁴⁰Then we seized this one and asked who the young man was, ⁴¹but she refused to tell us. We testify to this." The assembly believed them, since they were elders and judges of the people, and they condemned her to death.

⁴²But Susanna cried aloud: "Eternal God, you know what is hidden and are aware of all things before they come to be: ⁴³you know that they have testified falsely against me. Here I am about to die, though I have done none of the things for which these men have condemned me."

The trial is convened. Susanna appears with all her relatives for support. The accusers demand that she be unveiled so they can continue to inflame their lust even as they condemn her to death. Their fatal testimony is delivered. Both the men and Susanna are esteemed in the community. When the people are faced with a choice of whom to believe, the status of the men weighs more heavily than Susanna's virtue. They condemn Susanna to death. Susanna turns, not to any human defender, but to God. God knows the charges are false and will deliver her through Daniel.

Her Redeemer

Daniel 13:44-59

⁴⁴The Lord heard her prayer. ⁴⁵As she was being led to execution, God stirred up the holy spirit of a young boy named Daniel, ⁴⁶and he cried aloud: "I am innocent of this woman's blood." ⁴⁷All the people turned and asked him, "What are you saying?" ⁴⁸He stood in their midst and said, "Are you

such fools, you Israelites, to condemn a daughter of Israel without investigation and without clear evidence? [49]Return to court, for they have testified falsely against her."

[50]Then all the people returned in haste. To Daniel the elders said, "Come, sit with us and inform us, since God has given you the prestige of old age." [51]But he replied, "Separate these two far from one another, and I will examine them."

[52]After they were separated from each other, he called one of them and said: "How you have grown evil with age! Now have your past sins come to term: [53]passing unjust sentences, condemning the innocent, and freeing the guilty, although the Lord says, 'The innocent and the just you shall not put to death.' [54]Now, then, if you were a witness, tell me under what tree you saw them together." [55]"Under a mastic tree," he answered. "Your fine lie has cost you your head," said Daniel; "for the angel of God has already received the sentence from God and shall split you in two." [56]Putting him to one side, he ordered the other one to be brought. "Offspring of Canaan, not of Judah," Daniel said to him, "beauty has seduced you, lust has perverted your heart. [57]This is how you acted with the daughters of Israel, and in their fear they yielded to you; but a daughter of Judah did not tolerate your lawlessness. [58]Now, then, tell me under what tree you surprised them together." [59]"Under an oak," he said. "Your fine lie has cost you also your head," said Daniel; "for the angel of God waits with a sword to cut you in two so as to destroy you both."

God does not fail Susanna. But as usual God works through an unlikely human being to minister justice. God sends a young man to bring divine wisdom to the situation. Daniel demands that the case be reopened. He cross-examines the two elders separately and convicts them of false witness. Susanna is vindicated and delivered from death.

The story of Susanna exemplifies for every age the plight of the marginalized seeking **legal protection**. Just as Daniel became Susanna's advocate, calling for justice in a trial marred by corruption, we too are called upon to defend the defenseless, advocating for just laws and fair application of those laws. (See Isa 1:17; Jer 7:5-7; 21:12; Amos 5:15.)

Daniel 13:60-64

[60]The whole assembly cried aloud, blessing God who saves those who hope in him. [61]They rose up against the two old men, for by their own words Daniel had convicted them of bearing false witness. They condemned them to the fate they had planned for their neighbor: [62]in accordance with the law of Moses they put them to death. Thus was innocent blood spared that day.

[63]Hilkiah and his wife praised God for their daughter Susanna, with Joakim her husband and all her relatives, because she was found innocent of any shameful deed. [64]And from that day onward Daniel was greatly esteemed by the people.

The conclusion of the story restores the scene to its tranquility. The elders are condemned to the death they had plotted for Susanna. Susanna's reputation is restored, and the young Daniel gains great respect.

Susanna is an example of a virtuous woman who trusts God with her life. Her trust comes through in her two speeches in the narrative. The first declares her commitment to remain faithful to God and to her husband (13:22-23); the second is her cry to God for help (13:42-43). Both Susanna and Judith demonstrate courage and strength when confronted by enemies.

CONTINUING THE CONVERSATION

By Jaime L. Waters

Judith: Echoes of Biblical Women

Judith is one of the few books in the Bible named for a woman. It is one of the deuterocanonical books preserved in the Greek tradition of the Old Testament and is part of the biblical canon in the Catholic and Orthodox traditions.

Echoes of Deborah and Jael

Reading Judith with Deborah and Jael in mind can be edifying, as all three women are depicted as warriors, living during periods of unrest and taking strategic and violent actions in order to save the people of Israel. There are notable parallels and echoes between Judith 12–14 and Judges 4–5. The context is similar in that the Jews/Israelites are living in duress during periods of political struggle.

The interactions between Judith and Holofernes (Jdt 12-14) and Jael and Sisera (Judg 4-5) happen in domestic contexts—in particular, inside tents. Both military men presumably do not see these women as threats, as they do not see their attacks as forthcoming. When the men recline in their tents, Judith and Jael offer a false sense of hospitality and care, as Judith gives Holofernes food and wine and Jael gives Sisera milk. These gestures disarm the men and make them more susceptible to unforeseen attack.

Jael's actions feel less planned than Judith's, as the narrative and the song are relatively short in the description of the events. Readers do not get much insight into whether this was a premeditated action or a murder of opportunity. The book of Judith, on the other hand, describes the namesake of the book engaging in much more strategizing and prayer in anticipation of her act.

Both women have other women associated with them who affirm (Deborah) or encourage and facilitate (Judith's maid) their work. Likewise, both women target the head as a decisive attack point. Jael hammers a tent peg into Sisera's head, and Judith decapitates Holofernes. The traditions of Judges likely influenced the depiction of Judith.

Echoes of Other Biblical Women

Judith includes several other echoes of stories about biblical women. She is depicted as beautiful, using her beauty as a weapon within the larger narrative. The emphasis on women's beauty as a tool to seduce or as an explanation for why men are drawn to particular women is prominent in multiple biblical texts. For instance, Rachel, Bathsheba, and Susanna are noted for their beauty. Likewise, as you will see in Lesson Four, there are echoes of the book of Esther. Both women live during periods of foreign rule and use various characteristics and tactics such as beauty, banquets, and hospitality to exert influence.

Modern readers might struggle with the violent and gruesome imagery in Judith. Later artistic depictions of Judith frequently show her holding up Holofernes' head in victory. The original cover of Nowell's *Women in the Old Testament* depicted an image of Botticelli's Judith (see p. 63), including the decapitated head of Holofernes perched on the head of Judith's maid. This triumphant image might be offensive, but, in a way, it is an important reminder for readers to see women as complex, multidimensional characters. Judith, like Jael and Deborah, pushes us to think about the role of women as powerful and strategic warriors, making difficult choices and decisive moves for the betterment of themselves and their communities.

EXPLORING LESSON THREE

1. The historical underpinnings of the book of Judith could prove confusing since Israel's enemies, the Assyrians and the Babylonians, are rolled into one. How is this technique intended to enhance the story?

_____

_____

_____

_____

_____

2. In what ways does Judith "break the mold" of widows in the ancient world (Jdt 8:4-8; 16: 21-24)?

_____

_____

_____

_____

_____

3. Uzziah proclaims that Judith has good sense and is wise, prudent, and God-fearing (Jdt 8:28-31). Who are some other biblical figures who are described in this way? (See Exod 1:17; 1 Kgs 3:12; Job 1:1; Isa 11:2; Acts 7:9-10.)

_____

_____

_____

_____

_____

4. What feelings do you experience as you read the prayer Judith voices against her enemies (Jdt 9:7-14)? The psalmists often pray with the same blunt honesty (e.g., Pss 17:10-15; 59:10-18). What does this indicate to you about the nature of a person's or a community's relationship with God? Are there any parallels in your own prayer life?

_____

_____

_____

_____

_____

5. Judith credits the defeat of Holofernes to divine power and human planning (Jdt 13:4-5). When have you felt God's power working through your plans or the plans of others?

_____

_____

_____

_____

_____

_____

6. Susanna's firm conscience stands in stark contrast to the lack of a well-formed conscience in the two judges who attack her (Dan 13:9, 23). How do you nourish a healthy conscience or moral compass in your own life?

_____

_____

_____

_____

_____

_____

7. The people wrongly believed that the elders/judges were credible because of their status in the community (Dan 13:41). How do you evaluate whether a person is credible or has reliable character? (See Prov 4:20-23; Phil 4:8-9; 2 Pet 1:5-6.)

_____

_____

_____

_____

_____

8. In your experience, what situations have called forth in you or others the kind of faith and trust seen in Susanna?

_____

_____

_____

_____

9. Continuing the Conversation: In this essay, women warriors in Scripture are described as "powerful and strategic" women who made "difficult choices and decisive moves for the betterment of themselves and their communities." Do you know any women that you would describe as "warriors," not in literal terms of war or violence, but in their total dedication to the betterment of others?

_____

_____

_____

_____

_____

CLOSING PRAYER

Prayer

*"For the Lord is a God who crushes wars;
he sets his encampment among his people;
he delivered me from the hands of my
pursuers."* (Jdt 16:2)

Help us, O God, to know in the depth of our being that you are sovereign and powerful beyond our imagining. May we always be obedient to your word and fearless in doing your will. Give courage to all who are in danger, especially . . .

LESSON FOUR

Women in Power

Begin your personal study and group discussion with a simple and sincere prayer such as:

Prayer

You, O God, fill your people with courage, wisdom, and humility. Inspire us, as you inspired the women of Scripture, to use these virtues to transform the world.

Read pages 84–98, Lesson Four.

Respond to the questions on pages 99–101, Exploring Lesson Four.

The Closing Prayer on page 101 is for your personal use and may be used at the end of group discussion.

WOMEN IN POWER

Scripture excerpts are found in shaded text boxes throughout the lesson. For additional context, you may wish to read the full book of Esther.

The book of Esther has a unique biblical history. The Hebrew version never mentions the name of God. Perhaps for this reason the book was not accepted into the canon of the Hebrew Bible until the third century CE. It is the only book of the Hebrew Bible not found among the scrolls at Qumran. The Septuagint, the Greek translation of the Old Testament, contains several additions to the story which do make explicit mention of God.[5] These Greek additions are found in the Roman Catholic and Orthodox canon. Similar to the book of Daniel, Jewish and Protestant Bibles follow the shorter, Hebrew tradition.

The book of Esther is a story set in Persia during the fifth century BCE in which both the hero and the villain are painted in bold colors. In the Hebrew version of the story, the faithful Jews of the Diaspora, living outside of Israel, carry the hidden presence of God and are the ministers of God's providence. The Greek additions contain prayers addressed to God and an apocalyptic dream sequence explaining the Jews' vengeance on their enemies. What was subtly suggested in the Hebrew story is clearly stated in the Greek additions.

VASHTI

A Deposed Queen

Esther 1:1-22

[1]During the reign of Ahasuerus—the same Ahasuerus who ruled over a hundred and twenty-seven provinces from India to Ethiopia—[2]while he was occupying the royal throne in the royal precinct of Susa, [3]in the third year of his reign, he gave a feast for all his officials and ministers: the Persian and Median army officers, the nobles, and the governors of the provinces. [4]For as many as a hundred and eighty days, he displayed the glorious riches of his kingdom and the resplendent wealth of his royal estate.

[5]At the end of this time the king gave a feast of seven days in the garden court of the royal palace for all the people, great and small, who were in the royal precinct of Susa. [6]There were white cotton draperies and violet hangings, held by cords of fine crimson linen from silver rings on marble pillars. Gold and silver couches were on a mosaic pavement, which was of porphyry, marble, mother-of-pearl, and colored stones. [7]Drinks were served in a variety of golden cups, and the royal wine flowed freely, as befitted the king's liberality. [8]By ordinance of the king the drinking was unstinted, for he had instructed all the stewards of his household to comply with the good pleasure of everyone. [9]Queen Vashti also gave a feast for the women inside the royal palace of King Ahasuerus.

[10]On the seventh day, when the king was merry with wine, he instructed Mehuman, Biztha, Harbona, Bigtha, Abagtha, Zethar, and Carkas, the seven eunuchs who attended King Ahasuerus, [11]to bring Queen Vashti into his presence wearing the royal crown, that he might display her beauty to the populace and the officials, for she was lovely to behold. [12]But Queen Vashti refused to come at the royal order issued through the eunuchs. At

this the king's wrath flared up, and he burned with fury. [13]He conferred with the wise men versed in the law, because the king's business was conducted in general consultation with lawyers and jurists. [14]He summoned Carshena, Shethar, Admatha, Tarshish, Meres, Marsena and Memucan, the seven Persian and Median officials who were in the king's personal service and held first rank in the realm, [15]and asked them, "What is to be done by law with Queen Vashti for disobeying the order of King Ahasuerus issued through the eunuchs?"

[16]In the presence of the king and of the officials, Memucan answered: "Queen Vashti has not wronged the king alone, but all the officials and the populace throughout the provinces of King Ahasuerus. [17]For the queen's conduct will become known to all the women, and they will look with disdain upon their husbands when it is reported, 'King Ahasuerus commanded that Queen Vashti be ushered into his presence, but she would not come.' [18]This very day the Persian and Median ladies who hear of the queen's conduct will rebel against all the royal officials, with corresponding disdain and rancor. [19]If it please the king, let an irrevocable royal decree be issued by him and inscribed among the laws of the Persians and Medes, forbidding Vashti to come into the presence of King Ahasuerus and authorizing the king to give her royal dignity to one more worthy than she. [20]Thus, when the decree which the king will issue is published throughout his realm, vast as it is, all wives will honor their husbands, from the greatest to the least."

[21]This proposal found acceptance with the king and the officials, and the king acted on the advice of Memucan. [22]He sent letters to all the royal provinces, to each province in its own script and to each people in its own language, to the effect that every man should be lord in his own home.

The Persian court under Ahasuerus (Xerxes I, 485–464 BCE) is the scene of great wealth and high banqueting. The king holds a seven-day feast, and at the same time Queen Vashti holds a feast for the women. On the seventh and final day of the banquets, the king orders Vashti to appear at the men's banquet. He has displayed the rest of his wealth; now he desires to display the beauty of his queen.

Vashti is supposed to come "wearing the royal crown." There is a rabbinic tradition that she was supposed to come wearing nothing but the royal crown. It is unclear if this is the intention in the text, but this interpretation helps to explain Vashti's actions. Because her only function is to enhance the glory of the king, Vashti refuses to come. Her refusal creates a storm of protest among the king's advisers that goes far beyond the significance of the event. Their great fear is that Vashti's assertion of independence will encourage other wives to assert indepen-

 Exaggeration (or hyperbole) is a significant characteristic of the book of Esther. Everything is larger than life, as in these examples:

1:1	*"A hundred and twenty-seven provinces"*; actually about thirty provinces in the Persian empire at that time
1:4	Banquet lasting *180 days*
1:18-20	Since Vashti's disobedience will encourage *all* women to disobey their husbands, *all* women from greatest to least will be ordered to honor their husbands.
2:12	Beauty treatment lasting *twelve months* (six months with oil of myrrh, six months with perfume and cosmetics)
3:13; cf. 7:4; 8:11	Order to "destroy, kill and annihilate *all* the Jews . . . in *one* day"
5:14	A stake to impale Mordecai fifty cubits tall (seventy-five feet)

dence also. The absolute power of husbands over their wives will be in question.

The scene is a satire. Everything is exaggerated. The wealth is overwhelming. The banquets are celebrations of gluttony. The demand of the king is arbitrary. The response of the courtiers is overdrawn. The only sensible person in the scene seems to be Vashti. Nonetheless Vashti is deposed, and the stage is set for the search for a new queen.

ESTHER

Esther Arrives

Esther 2:1-7

[1]After this, when King Ahasuerus' wrath had cooled, he thought over what Vashti had done and what had been decreed against her. [2]Then the king's personal attendants suggested: "Let beautiful young virgins be sought for the king. [3]Let the king appoint commissaries in all the provinces of his realm to bring together all beautiful young virgins to the harem in the stronghold of Susa. Under the care of the royal eunuch Hegai, custodian of the women, let cosmetics be given them. [4]Then the girl who pleases the king shall reign in place of Vashti." This suggestion pleased the king, and he acted accordingly.

[5]There was in the stronghold of Susa a certain Jew named Mordecai, son of Jair, son of Shimei, son of Kish, a Benjaminite, [6]who had been exiled from Jerusalem with the captives taken with Jeconiah, king of Judah, whom Nebuchadnezzar, king of Babylon, had deported. [7]He was foster father to Hadassah, that is, Esther, his cousin; for she had lost both father and mother. The girl was beautifully formed and lovely to behold. On the death of her father and mother, Mordecai had taken her as his own daughter.

Esther is introduced in the context of the search for a queen. She is a Jew, an orphan, and very beautiful. Her Hebrew name is Hadassah, the myrtle plant, symbol of thanksgiving and peace. Her Persian name, Esther, is a variant of

Ishtar, the Babylonian goddess of fertility. She has been adopted by her cousin Mordecai, who has become her protector.

Esther 2:8-11

[8]When the king's order and decree had been obeyed and many maidens brought together to the stronghold of Susa under the care of Hegai, Esther also was brought in to the royal palace under the care of Hegai, custodian of the women. [9]The girl pleased him and won his favor. So he promptly furnished her with cosmetics and provisions. Then picking out seven maids for her from the royal palace, he transferred both her and her maids to the best place in the harem. [10]Esther did not reveal her nationality or family, for Mordecai had commanded her not to do so.

[11]Day by day Mordecai would walk about in front of the court of the harem, to learn how Esther was faring and what was to become of her.

Esther and Ahasuerus

Esther is not only beautiful; she also has a pleasing personality. She immediately wins the favor of the eunuch Hegai who is put in charge of the harem. His assistance will prove invaluable to her. She seems docile as she participates in the beauty treatments preparing her to go to the king. But as the story progresses, she will act assertively. She conceals her Jewish identity, which sets up the conflict of the story. Her revelation to the king that she is a Jew will be the turning point of the plot.

The Beauty Contest

Esther 2:12-18

¹²After the twelve months' preparation decreed for the women, each one went in turn to visit King Ahasuerus. During this period of beautifying treatment, six months were spent with oil of myrrh, and the other six months with perfumes and cosmetics. ¹³Then, when each one was to visit the king, she was allowed to take with her from the harem to the royal palace whatever she chose. ¹⁴She would go in the evening and return in the morning to a second harem under the care of the royal eunuch Shaashgaz, guardian of the concubines. She could not return to the king unless he was pleased with her and had her summoned by name. ¹⁵As for Esther, daughter of Abihail and adopted daughter of his nephew Mordecai, when her turn came to visit the king, she did not ask for anything but what the royal eunuch Hegai, guardian of the women, suggested. And she won the admiration of all who saw her.

¹⁶Esther was led to King Ahasuerus in his palace in the tenth month, Tebeth, in the seventh year of his reign. ¹⁷The king loved Esther more than all other women, and of all the virgins she won his favor and good will. So he placed the royal crown on her head and made her queen in place of Vashti. ¹⁸Then the king gave a great feast in honor of Esther to all his officials and servants, granting a holiday to the provinces and bestowing gifts with royal generosity.

The preparation for this royal beauty contest lasts a whole year. Esther participates along with the other young women in the anointings and instructions in the use of perfumes and cosmetics. There is a great emphasis on external beauty.

When Esther is taken in to the king, she relies completely on the advice of Hegai. She trusts him to know what will please the king. Her beauty is admired by all who see her. The king's decision affirms their opinion. The king is won over by Esther and names her queen in place of Vashti.

Esther has won the favor (*hesed*) of the eunuch Hegai (2:9) and the admiration or good will (*hen*) of the people (2:15). She has won the favor and good will (*hesed* and *hen*) of the king (2:17). This phrase is a clue to what will happen later in the story. She is like Joseph, who found favor (*hen*) in the sight of Potiphar and brought blessing to his house (Gen 39:4). God also showed kindness (*hesed*) to Joseph by giving him favor (*hen*) in the sight of the chief jailer, and brought success to all that he did (Gen 39:21). She is like Ruth, a woman of faithful love (*hesed*, Ruth 3:10), who finds favor (*hen*) in the sight of Boaz (Ruth 2:10, 13) and brings blessing to his house. Esther will again win the favor (*hen*) of the king and will be able to save her people (5:2, 8; 7:3; 8:5).

At this point in the story, however, Esther's character has not yet been revealed. Has the king simply replaced a beautiful, independent queen with a beautiful, docile queen? Will Esther make any difference in the life of Persia or in the lives of her fellow Jews?

Impending Danger

Esther 2:19-23

¹⁹As was said, from the time the virgins had been brought together, and while Mordecai was passing his time at the king's gate, ²⁰Esther had not revealed her family or nationality, because

continue

Mordecai had told her not to; and Esther continued to follow Mordecai's instructions, just as she had when she was being brought up by him. [21]During the time that Mordecai spent at the king's gate, Bigthan and Teresh, two of the royal eunuchs who guarded the entrance, became angry and plotted to assassinate King Ahasuerus. [22]When the plot became known to Mordecai, he told Queen Esther, who in turn informed the king in Mordecai's name. [23]The matter was investigated and verified, and both of them were impaled on stakes. This was written in the annals in the king's presence.

The first clue to the difference that Esther will make comes in a note concerning Mordecai's discovery of a plot to assassinate the king. Mordecai reports the plot to Esther, who in turn informs the king, acting as an intermediary. The traitors are executed, and the affair is recorded in the royal annals. Later in the story, the king's rediscovery of Mordecai's act will bring the conflict between Mordecai (the Jew) and Haman (their enemy) to a head (6:1-11).

The conflict between Mordecai and Haman is described in chapter three. Haman, raised to high rank by the king, demands that all the king's servants at the royal gate kneel and bow down to him. Mordecai refuses to do so. The reason he gives is that he is a Jew. Presumably he is making the point that he bows to God alone. Haman, enraged by Mordecai's refusal to bow to him, seeks an opportunity to destroy all the Jews in Ahasuerus' kingdom. He persuades the king to issue a decree that on a single day all the Jews of the kingdom should be killed. The day, chosen by lot (9:24-26), is the thirteenth day of the twelfth month, the month of Adar.

Esther 4:1-9

[1]When Mordecai learned all that was happening, he tore his garments, put on sackcloth and ashes, and went through the city crying out loudly and bitterly, [2]till he came before the royal gate, which no one clothed in sackcloth might enter. [3]Likewise in each of the provinces, wherever the king's decree and law reached, the Jews went into deep mourning, with fasting, weeping, and lament; most of them lay on sackcloth and ashes.

[4]Esther's maids and eunuchs came and told her. Overwhelmed with anguish, the queen sent garments for Mordecai to put on, so that he might take off his sackcloth; but he refused. [5]Esther then summoned Hathach, one of the king's eunuchs whom he had placed at her service, and commanded him to find out what this action of Mordecai meant and the reason for it. [6]So Hathach went out to Mordecai in the public square in front of the royal gate, [7]and Mordecai recounted all that had happened to him, as well as the exact amount of silver Haman had promised to pay to the royal treasury for the slaughter of the Jews. [8]He also gave him a copy of the written decree for their destruction that had been promulgated in Susa, to show and explain to Esther. Hathach was to instruct her to go to the king and to plead and intercede with him on behalf of her people.

[9]Hathach returned to Esther and told her what Mordecai had said.

Esther's transformation begins in chapter four. First of all, she seems embarrassed by Mordecai's sackcloth and ashes. Without determining the reason for his penance, she attempts to end his public display. It is also evident that the news of the royal decree authorizing the slaughter of the Jews has reached the provinces but has not reached the queen. She is not privy to the king's decisions, nor is she provided with the ordinary news of the kingdom.

It is Mordecai, through Hathach, who must inform Esther of the impending danger. He suggests that she, too, is in danger; he refers to "her people." He also gives her instructions. She is to plead both with the king and with God. Esther gains information and direction from Mordecai.

For a Time Like This

Esther 4:10-17

[10]Then Esther replied to Hathach and gave him this message for Mordecai: [11]"All the servants of the king and the people of his provinces know that any man or woman who goes to the king in the inner court without being summoned is subject to the same law—death. Only if the king extends the golden scepter will such a person live. Now as for me, I have not been summoned to the king for thirty days."

[12]When Esther's words were reported to Mordecai, [13]he had this reply brought to her: "Do not imagine that you are safe in the king's palace, you alone of all the Jews. [14]Even if you now remain silent, relief and deliverance will come to the Jews from another source; but you and your father's house will perish. Who knows—perhaps it was for a time like this that you became queen?"

[15]Esther sent back to Mordecai the response: [16]"Go and assemble all the Jews who are in Susa; fast on my behalf, all of you, not eating or drinking night or day for three days. I and my maids will also fast in the same way. Thus prepared, I will go to the king, contrary to the law. If I perish, I perish!" [17]Mordecai went away and did exactly as Esther had commanded.

Through her messenger Hathach, Esther begins a dialogue with Mordecai. She is reluctant to go to the king, fearing death for appearing before him unsummoned. She may also remember the consequences of Vashti's disobedience. Her own relationship with the king may be cooling. He has not sent for her in a month. It also seems that she has not fully realized the danger to herself.

Mordecai is not deterred by Esther's fear, nor will he allow her to ignore her own Jewish roots. With strong words he exhorts her to act. He reminds her that she faces death in any case: death for approaching the king, or death as a Jew if she does not approach him. His final word is a testimony to divine providence: "Who knows—perhaps it was for a time like this that you became queen?" Esther is not queen for her own sake; God has raised her to this position in order to use her as a savior of her people. In this she is reminiscent of Joseph, who was sold into slavery and raised to high position in order to be the savior of many people (Gen 50:20).

Mordecai's words persuade Esther. At this moment she takes charge of her own destiny. She will accept the task set before her. She begins her preparation by declaring her intent to fast and asking for the supportive fast of all her people. She faces the possibility of death with courage.

Esther did not fast alone but requested that the Jewish people fast for and with her and her maids (4:16). **Fasting** was a common spiritual practice in Israel, associated with mourning the death of a loved one (1 Sam 31:11-13), asking God for a personal favor (2 Sam 12:15-16), seeking guidance in a time of national crisis (2 Chron 20:1-4; Esth 4:16), or expressing repentance as a community (Neh 9:1).

The fundamental idea communicated by fasting was humility, indicated in the use of the Hebrew word *ta'anit* (from a root word meaning "humility" or "affliction"), which describes such rituals. An intentional act of humility in a society that valued honor so highly would likely receive attention from others; the prayerful humility of fasting was intended to secure God's attention and assistance.

Esther's Prayer

Esther C:12-30

[12]Queen Esther, seized with mortal anguish, fled to the Lord for refuge. [13]Taking off her splendid garments, she put on garments of distress and
continue

mourning. In place of her precious ointments she covered her head with dung and ashes. She afflicted her body severely and in place of her festive adornments, her tangled hair covered her.

¹⁴Then she prayed to the Lord, the God of Israel, saying: "My Lord, you alone are our King. Help me, who am alone and have no help but you, ¹⁵for I am taking my life in my hand. ¹⁶From birth, I have heard among my people that you, Lord, chose Israel from among all nations, and our ancestors from among all their forebears, as a lasting inheritance, and that you fulfilled all your promises to them. ¹⁷But now we have sinned in your sight, and you have delivered us into the hands of our enemies, ¹⁸because we worshiped their gods. You are just, O Lord. ¹⁹But now they are not satisfied with our bitter servitude, but have sworn an oath to their idols ²⁰to do away with the decree you have pronounced, to destroy your inheritance, to close the mouths of those who praise you, to extinguish the glory of your house and your altar, ²¹to open the mouths of the nations to acclaim their worthless gods, and to extol a mortal king forever.

²²"Lord, do not relinquish your scepter to those who are nothing. Do not let our foes gloat over our ruin, but turn their own counsel against them and make an example of the one who began this against us. ²³Be mindful of us, Lord. Make yourself known in the time of our distress and give me courage, King of gods and Ruler of every power. ²⁴Put in my mouth persuasive words in the presence of the lion, and turn his heart to hatred for our enemy, so that he and his co-conspirators may perish. ²⁵Save us by your power, and help me, who am alone and have no one but you, Lord.

²⁶"You know all things. You know that I hate the pomp of the lawless, and abhor the bed of the uncircumcised or of any foreigner. ²⁷You know that I am under constraint, that I abhor the sign of grandeur that rests on my head when I appear in public. I abhor it like a polluted rag, and do not wear it in private. ²⁸I, your servant, have never eaten at the table of Haman, nor have I graced the banquet of the king or drunk the wine of libations. ²⁹From the day I was brought here till now, your

servant has had no joy except in you, Lord, God of Abraham. ³⁰O God, whose power is over all, hear the voice of those in despair. Save us from the power of the wicked, and deliver me from my fear."

The content of Esther's prayer is found only in the Greek additions of Esther, which expand the Hebrew story and make explicit its veiled references to God.

The queen, who had attempted to dissuade Mordecai from his penitential display, now herself puts on sackcloth and ashes and begins to pray. She interweaves the traditional elements of a lament. She addresses her cry directly to God, who alone can help her. She describes her distress: "I am taking my life in my hand." She praises God: "You are just, O Lord." She tries to motivate God to act: "[Y]ou, Lord, chose Israel from among all nations." She begs God to help her: "Save us by your power, and help me, who am alone and have no one but you, Lord." The whole prayer is a testimony to her faith and to her recognition that all power belongs to God.

She persuades God with a reminder of God's faithfulness to Israel in past ages and acknowledges God's justice in sending the people into exile. She is certain, however, that the total extermination of the covenant people is not God's desire. So she persuades further. If God allows the destruction of the Jews, God will be surrendering power to an earthly ruler. She underlines her point with the titles, "King of gods and Ruler of every power." Then she returns to her petition that God, who alone can help her, will give her the weapon of persuasive words.

Finally Esther focuses on herself. She declares her worthiness to act as God's minister in this act of salvation. She has been faithful to her Jewish tradition; she does not glory in the pomp of the court. Her only joy is in God. Esther's prayer ends with a petition for God to hear, save, and deliver her from her fear.

At Risk of Her Life

Esther D

¹On the third day, ending her prayers, she took off her prayer garments and arrayed herself in her splendid attire. ²In making her appearance, after invoking the all-seeing God and savior, she took with her two maids; ³on the one she leaned gently for support, ⁴while the other followed her, bearing her train. ⁵She glowed with perfect beauty and her face was as joyous as it was lovely, though her heart was pounding with fear. ⁶She passed through all the portals till she stood before the king, who was seated on his royal throne, clothed in full robes of state, and covered with gold and precious stones, so that he inspired great awe. ⁷As he looked up in extreme anger, his features fiery and majestic, the queen staggered, turned pale and fainted, collapsing against the maid in front of her. ⁸But God changed the king's anger to gentleness. In great anxiety he sprang from his throne, held her in his arms until she recovered, and comforted her with reassuring words. ⁹"What is it, Esther?" he said to her. "I am your brother. Take courage! ¹⁰You shall not die; this order of ours applies only to our subjects. ¹¹Come near!" ¹²Raising the golden scepter, he touched her neck with it, embraced her, and said, "Speak to me."

¹³She replied: "I saw you, my lord, as an angel of God, and my heart was shaken by fear of your majesty. ¹⁴For you are awesome, my lord, though your countenance is full of mercy." ¹⁵As she said this, she fainted. ¹⁶The king was shaken and all his attendants tried to revive her.

Esther 5

¹[Now on the third day, Esther put on her royal garments and stood in the inner courtyard, looking toward the royal palace, while the king was seated on his royal throne in the audience chamber, facing the palace doorway. ²When he saw Queen Esther standing in the courtyard, she won his favor and he extended toward her the golden scepter he held. She came up to him, and touched the top of the scepter.]

³Then the king said to her, "What is it, Queen Esther? What is your request? Even if it is half of my kingdom, it shall be granted you." ⁴Esther replied, "If it please your majesty, come today with Haman to a banquet I have prepared." ⁵The king ordered, "Have Haman make haste to fulfill the wish of Esther."

So the king went with Haman to the banquet Esther had prepared. ⁶During the drinking of the wine, the king said to Esther, "Whatever you ask for shall be granted, and whatever request you make shall be honored, even if it is for half my kingdom." ⁷Esther replied: "This is my petition and request: ⁸if I have found favor with the king and if it pleases your majesty to grant my petition and honor my request, let the king come with Haman tomorrow to a banquet I will prepare; and tomorrow I will do as the king asks."

⁹That day Haman left happy and in good spirits. But when he saw that Mordecai at the royal gate did not rise, and showed no fear of him, he was filled with anger toward him. ¹⁰Haman restrained himself, however, and went home, where he summoned his friends and his wife Zeresh. ¹¹He recounted the greatness of his riches, the large number of his sons, and how the king had promoted him and placed him above the officials and royal servants. ¹²"Moreover," Haman added, "Queen Esther invited no one but me to come with the king to the banquet she prepared; again tomorrow I am to be her guest with the king. ¹³Yet none of this satisfies me as long as I continue to see the Jew Mordecai sitting at the royal gate." ¹⁴His wife Zeresh and all his friends said to him, "Have a stake set up, fifty cubits in height, and in the morning ask the king to have Mordecai impaled on it. Then go to the banquet with the king in good spirits." This suggestion pleased Haman, and he had the stake erected.

There are notable differences between the Hebrew and Greek traditions regarding how Esther approaches the king. In the Hebrew version (5:1-5) Esther, dressed in her royal garments, is simply welcomed by the king when he sees her approach. In the Greek version (D:1-15) the encounter has been made much more dramatic through a series of comparisons and contrasts. Esther's penitential garments are replaced by her royal attire. She appeals to God before going to appeal to the king. The beauty of Esther's face compares to the regal splendor of the king's appearance. The fire of the king's rage contrasts with the queen's pallor. God comes to Esther's rescue by changing the king's anger to gentleness.

The Hebrew version continues with the conversation between the king and Esther. She does not ask for half the kingdom as the king suggests, nor does she ask for the rescue of her people. She simply invites the king to come with Haman to a banquet. The simplicity of her request veils the seriousness of her purpose. She carries out God's mission of saving the people, not by military exploits or prophetic preaching, but through an invitation to a meal.

At the first banquet that Esther prepares for the king and Haman (5:4-8), the king swears a second time to grant whatever Esther wishes, even half the kingdom. She requests only that the two men come to a second banquet. The delay serves the dramatic purpose of heightening the tension. We are left to wonder if Esther has lost her nerve, if she is testing the king's devotion to her, or if she is waiting for Haman to make a foolish move. There is no answer; we, too, must wait for the second banquet.

Between the banquets the conflict between Mordecai and Haman intensifies (5:9–6:14). Haman's volatile nature is revealed by violent mood swings. He is puffed up by the invitation to the queen's second banquet; he is distraught over Mordecai's repeated refusal to honor him. His wife suggests that he prepare a giant gibbet (a scaffold about seventy-five feet high with a pole) and ask the king to have Mordecai hanged (or impaled) on it. This restores his good humor, but his troubles are not over.

That same night the king, unable to sleep, has the royal chronicles read to him. He hears the story of Mordecai's report of the plot against the king (see 2:19-23) and discovers that nothing has been done for Mordecai. So the next day he asks Haman how a loyal servant should be rewarded. Haman, thinking that the king is speaking of him, describes a public display of honor. The king sends him out to honor Mordecai according to his description. A humiliated Haman tells his troubles to his wife, who predicts that he will be defeated by Mordecai. Haman then prepares to attend the second royal banquet.

Esther's Request

Esther 7:1-8

[1]So the king and Haman went to the banquet with Queen Esther. [2]Again, on this second day, as they were drinking wine, the king said to Esther, "Whatever you ask, Queen Esther, shall be granted you. Whatever request you make, even for half the kingdom, shall be honored." [3]Queen Esther replied: "If I have found favor with you, O king, and if it pleases your majesty, I ask that my life be spared, and I beg that you spare the lives of my people. [4]For we have been sold, I and my people, to be destroyed, killed, and annihilated. If we were only to be sold into slavery I would remain silent, for then our distress would not have been worth troubling the king." [5]King Ahasuerus said to Queen Esther, "Who and where is the man who has dared to do this?" [6]Esther replied, "The enemy oppressing us is this wicked Haman." At this, Haman was seized with dread of the king and queen.

[7]The king left the banquet in anger and went into the garden of the palace, but Haman stayed to beg Queen Esther for his life, since he saw that the king had decided on his doom. [8]When the king returned from the palace garden to the banquet hall, Haman had thrown himself on the couch on which Esther was reclining; and the king exclaimed, "Will he also violate the queen while she is with me in my own house!" Scarcely had the king spoken when the face of Haman was covered over.

The story of Esther revolves around the threat of **genocide**, first of the Jewish inhabitants of Persia and Media, and then of the enemies of the Jewish people. Genocide seeks to eradicate all or a substantial number of an identified national, ethnic, racial, or religious group. The Vatican II document, *Gaudium et Spes*, includes genocide in its list of infamies that poison human society and dishonor the Creator (27).

At the second banquet the king repeats the offer he made at the first banquet: "Whatever you ask, Queen Esther, shall be granted you." This is now the third time that the king has offered Esther as much as half the kingdom. Finally, Esther presents her petition: "I ask that my life be spared, and I beg that you spare the lives of my people."

The king is astounded and demands to know the name of the enemy who plans to do this dreadful thing. Esther names Haman, who is overcome by dread. He has fatally underestimated the strength of those whom he planned to destroy. This folly will mean his own destruction.

Esther accuses Haman. Gustave Dore (1870)

Haman thinks he has only one chance to escape death. He appeals to the one whom he recognizes as most powerful with the king, Esther. The method of his appeal, however, seals his fate. The king sees his prostrate form on Esther's couch, not as desperate submission, but as the threat of rape: "Will he also violate the queen while she is with me in my own house!" The verb *kabash*, translated here as "violate," also means "rape." Haman's indiscretion removes all hope; his face is described as "covered over," as if he were already dead.

Reversals

Esther 7:9–8:12

[9]Harbona, one of the eunuchs who attended the king, said, "At the house of Haman stands a stake fifty cubits high. Haman made it for Mordecai, who gave the report that benefited the king." The king answered, "Impale him on it." [10]So they impaled Haman on the stake he had set up for Mordecai, and the anger of the king abated.

[8:1]That day King Ahasuerus gave the house of Haman, enemy of the Jews, to Queen Esther; and Mordecai was admitted to the king's presence, for Esther had revealed his relationship to her. [2]The king removed his signet ring that he had taken away from Haman, and gave it to Mordecai; and Esther put Mordecai in charge of the house of Haman.

[3]Esther again spoke to the king. She fell at his feet and tearfully implored him to revoke the harm done by Haman the Agagite and the plan he had devised against the Jews. [4]The king stretched forth the golden scepter to Esther. So she rose and, standing before him, [5]said: "If it seems good to the king and if I have found favor with him, if the thing seems right to the king and I am pleasing in his eyes, let a document be issued to revoke the letters that the schemer Haman, son of Hammedatha the Agagite, wrote for the destruction of the Jews in all the royal provinces. [6]For how can I

continue

witness the evil that is to befall my people, and how can I behold the destruction of my kindred?"

[7]King Ahasuerus then said to Queen Esther and to the Jew Mordecai: "Now that I have given Esther the house of Haman, and they have impaled him on the stake because he was going to attack the Jews, [8]you in turn may write in the king's name what you see fit concerning the Jews and seal the letter with the royal signet ring." For a decree written in the name of the king and sealed with the royal signet ring cannot be revoked.

[9]At that time, on the twenty-third day of the third month, Sivan, the royal scribes were summoned. Exactly as Mordecai dictated, they wrote to the Jews and to the satraps, governors, and officials of the hundred and twenty-seven provinces from India to Ethiopia: to each province in its own script and to each people in its own language, and to the Jews in their own script and language. [10]These letters, which he wrote in the name of King Ahasuerus and sealed with the royal signet ring, he sent by mounted couriers riding thoroughbred royal steeds. [11]In these letters the king authorized the Jews in each and every city to gather and defend their lives, to destroy, kill, and annihilate every armed group of any nation or province that might attack them, along with their wives and children, and to seize their goods as spoil [12]on a single day throughout the provinces of King Ahasuerus, the thirteenth day of the twelfth month, Adar.

In his irrational anger against Mordecai, Haman has unwittingly prepared for his own execution. The king decrees that Haman be hanged. His house is given to Esther; Mordecai replaces him as keeper of the king's signet ring. Through Esther's influence, the roles of Haman and Mordecai are completely reversed.

Esther's major purpose, however, is still not resolved. According to the story the royal decrees of Persia are irrevocable. Thus the decree to slaughter the Jews still stands, even after Haman is dead. So Esther risks a second approach to the king. After he has welcomed her, she unveils a plan to counteract the decree. The king continues to give Esther whatever

she wishes. He empowers her to write a second irrevocable decree in his name and sealed with his signet ring. Mordecai dictates the new decree that authorizes the Jews to defend themselves against the slaughter commanded by the first decree.

Esther 9:11-15

[11]On the same day, when the number of those killed in the royal precinct of Susa was reported to the king, [12]he said to Queen Esther: "In the royal precinct of Susa the Jews have killed and destroyed five hundred people, as well as the ten sons of Haman. What must they have done in the other royal provinces! You shall again be granted whatever you ask, and whatever you request shall be honored." [13]So Esther said, "If it pleases your majesty, let the Jews in Susa be permitted again tomorrow to act according to today's decree, and let the ten sons of Haman be impaled on stakes." [14]The king then gave an order that this be done, and the decree was published in Susa. So the ten sons of Haman were impaled, [15]and the Jews in Susa mustered again on the fourteenth of the month of Adar and killed three hundred people in Susa. However, they did not engage in plundering.

Still the story does not end. Once more the king promises Esther whatever she requests. Once more a decree is issued according to Esther's wishes, granting the Jews authority to defend themselves against their enemies. Once more Esther is the source of power for the people.

Feast of Purim

Esther 9:24-32

[24]Haman, son of Hammedatha the Agagite, the foe of all the Jews, had planned to destroy

them and had cast the *pur*, or lot, for the time of their defeat and destruction. ²⁵Yet, when the plot became known to the king, the king ordered in writing that the wicked plan Haman had devised against the Jews should instead be turned against Haman and that he and his sons should be impaled on stakes. ²⁶And so these days have been named Purim after the word *pur*.

Thus, because of all that was contained in this letter, and because of what they had witnessed and experienced in this event, ²⁷the Jews established and adopted as a custom for themselves, their descendants, and all who should join them, the perpetual obligation of celebrating these two days every year in the manner prescribed by this letter, and at the time appointed. ²⁸These days were to be commemorated and kept in every generation, by every clan, in every province, and in every city. These days of Purim were never to be neglected among the Jews, nor forgotten by their descendants.

²⁹Queen Esther, daughter of Abihail, and Mordecai the Jew, wrote to confirm with full authority this second letter about Purim, ³⁰and Mordecai sent documents concerning peace and security to all the Jews in the hundred and twenty-seven provinces of Ahasuerus' kingdom. ³¹Thus were established, for their appointed time, these days of Purim which Mordecai the Jew and Queen Esther had designated for the Jews, just as they had previously enjoined upon themselves and upon their descendants the duty of fasting and supplication. ³²The command of Esther confirmed these prescriptions for Purim and was recorded in the book.

In this chapter the story of Esther is used to explain the foundation of the Jewish festival of Purim. Just as the spring rituals of non-Israelite farmers and shepherds were given a historical context and shaped into the festival of Passover in order to memorialize God's deliverance of the people at the exodus, so also the Babylonian festival celebrating the reversal of fates at the New Year is given a Jewish story in order to memorialize God's salvation of the good (Mordecai) and punishment of the wicked (Haman).

The Babylonian word *puru-um*, meaning "lot" or "fate," is related to the Hebrew word *purim*, meaning "lots." The name of the feast, Purim, is then connected to Haman's casting of lots to determine the date for the slaughter of the Jews.

The Jewish festival of Purim is celebrated on the fourteenth to fifteenth of the month of Adar (February–March), the last month of the Jewish calendar (or in Adar Sheni during a leap year). It is a celebratory feast that commemorates the saving of Jewish people during the Persian period. Purim is celebrated with actions such as exchanging gifts like food and wine, feasting, charitable donations, wearing costumes, public praying, and reading the book of Esther.

Esther, identified here as queen and as the biological daughter of Abihail and the adopted daughter of Mordecai, is portrayed as the authority who promulgates the celebration of Purim. She and Mordecai establish the proper days and practices for the feast.

 The yearly celebration of the **Feast of Purim** (also known as the Feast of Lots) includes a ritual reading of the book of Esther, with loud voices and noisemakers used to drown out every mention of Haman's name. One of the symbols of Purim is the "grogger" (a noisemaker much like a rattler).

Savior of Her People

Esther F

¹Then Mordecai said: "This is the work of God. ²I recall the dream I had about these very things, and not a single detail has been left unfulfilled— ³the tiny spring that grew into a river, and there was light, and sun, and many waters. The river is Esther, whom the king married and made queen. ⁴The two dragons are myself and Haman.

continue

⁵The nations are those who assembled to destroy the name of the Jews, ⁶but my people is Israel, who cried to God and was saved.

"The Lord saved his people and delivered us from all these evils. God worked signs and great wonders, such as have not occurred among the nations. ⁷For this purpose he arranged two lots: one for the people of God, the second for all the other nations. ⁸These two lots were fulfilled in the hour, the time, and the day of judgment before God and among all the nations. ⁹God remembered his people and rendered justice to his inheritance.

¹⁰"Gathering together with joy and happiness before God, they shall celebrate these days on the fourteenth and fifteenth of the month Adar throughout all future generations of his people Israel."

¹¹In the fourth year of the reign of Ptolemy and Cleopatra, Dositheus, who said he was a priest and Levite, and his son Ptolemy brought the present letter of Purim, saying that it was genuine and that Lysimachus, son of Ptolemy, of the community of Jerusalem, had translated it.

There is a final Greek addition to the book of Esther which, like the first addition, describes a dream of Mordecai. In the first description of the dream (A:4-10), Mordecai sees two dragons poised for combat. The battle of these two enemies threatens the just people of the world with destruction. When the just cry out to God, a little spring becomes a great river. The sun comes out and the lowly devour those who are honored. Mordecai's dream is interpreted in the final Greek addition (F:1-10). The little spring that becomes a great river is Esther, the queen. Her becoming great is the beginning of the salvation of the people.

The story of Esther is the story of a young Jewish woman who is raised to great power. Initially she is passive, accepting the instructions and guidance of others, submitting to whatever is expected of her. The threatened destruction of her people is the crisis that helps her adapt and develop. She heeds the words of her adoptive father and mentor Mordecai: "Who knows—perhaps it was for a time like this that you became queen?" The full strength of her character appears in her courageous approach to the king to plead for her people. The depth of her wisdom is revealed in her patient arrangement of circumstances that will assure a favorable answer from the king.

At the end of the story Esther has reached her full power as a faithful Jewish woman and the Persian queen. She exercises both political and liturgical authority. Through her, God has once again restored the life of the covenant people.

CONTINUING THE CONVERSATION

By Jaime L. Waters

Vashti: A Power of Her Own

Much of the book of Esther focuses on the book's namesake and her actions to save Jewish people living in the Persian Empire. Queen Esther is obviously one of the central characters of the book, but we should not overlook the role of Queen Vashti at its beginning. Vashti's act of refusal is an amazing affront, especially in a context in which men were often given power over women and their bodies. Vashti is a biblical example of a woman who controls and protects her own body, and she should be remembered and appreciated for that act.

Vashti's Refusal

In Esther 1, the Persian King Ahasuerus holds a lavish feast: "Drinks were served in a variety of golden cups, and the royal wine flowed freely, as befitted the king's liberality. By ordinance of the king the drinking was unstinted, for he had instructed all the stewards of his household to comply with the good pleasure of everyone" (1:7-8). This is clearly an over-the-top party with mandated, free-flowing alcohol. While the king's feast goes on, Vashti holds a women's banquet which shows her status and power in the empire. These dual banquets are an indication of wealth at an excessive level, and these parties give us an exaggerated image of privilege and luxury that might have characterized royal court life.

As the text continues, the boozy king sends royal eunuchs to bring Vashti to show off her beauty to the king and the other men at the banquet. Vashti refuses, and her refusal angers the king and prompts him to seek counsel. The king's advisors say that Vashti's actions are wrong, and they fear that Vashti could inspire other women: "For the queen's conduct will become known to all the women, and they will look with disdain upon their husbands" (1:17a). The advisors tell Ahasuerus that reprimanding Vashti through a royal decree will ensure that women will honor their husbands. Accordingly, the king issues a decree in every province's language that "every man should be lord in his own house" (1:22b).

Exploring Vashti's Motives

Nowell characterizes this text as satirical, and the extremes are almost laughable if not for the realities that undergird them. Vashti's refusal is notable for a few important reasons. The passage does not tell us why she refuses to comply with the king's request. Perhaps she simply did not want to go. Perhaps she didn't want to leave her own banquet, or perhaps she recognized the risks of attending the men's banquet. Because the text leaves readers wondering, it has inspired some interpreters and traditions to posit that the king wanted Vashti to attend the party "wearing the royal crown" and nothing else, meaning he wanted her to arrive at the party naked.

Vashti's refusal may have been for her own safety. The king wants to ogle and show off Vashti's beauty while heavily drinking with other men at a private party. Consider Vashti's actions in light of the stories of Susanna (see Lesson Three) and Bathsheba and Tamar (see Lesson One). The beauty of women on display to men can sometimes lead to coercion, harassment, and sexual assault. Biblical narratives depict such risks; unfortunately, these concerns persist today. Vashti's refusal might have cost her the royal title, but it also protected her from possible sexual assault, the risk of which was only heightened by the drunkenness at the banquet.

The Power of Inspiration

Another notable detail is found in the response to Vashti's refusal. The men in the narrative fear that other women might now rebel against their husbands. In an extreme response, they attempt to quell rebellion through royal decree. Their action reveals a norm that women should acquiesce to men in society, especially their husbands. Vashti's refusal is offensive to her husband and to all men. The men are depicted as seeing the power of one woman's refusal and then worrying that Vashti's action could interrupt the norm. Other women may feel empowered and emboldened to take more control over themselves and their bodies.

Some interpreters compare Vashti and Esther, showing ways that Esther also upends the system, but in more subtle, demure, and effective ways. But we need not pit these two women characters against each other. Vashti is not simply a literary foil for Esther, although themes and events in Vashti's story set the stage for Esther's story. Vashti, in her own right, gives readers another perspective on royal women in the Persian period. While Vashti does not maintain her royal power, she does maintain power over her body, and for that she is both memorable and inspirational.

EXPLORING LESSON FOUR

1. The king's officials saw Queen Vashti's refusal to come when summoned by the king as an affront to his position as husband and ruler (1:17-22), and they feared other women would assert themselves in challenging ways. In what areas do you notice that the roles of men and women are still evolving? How do you feel about and respond to some of these changes?

_____

_____

_____

_____

_____

_____

2. Once she was called to court, Esther sometimes hid her Jewish identity (2:10, 20) and sometimes took advantage of it (4:8; B:8-9). Why did she hide it at first? How did she, in the end, rely on it and reveal it?

_____

_____

_____

_____

3. How did Mordecai convince Esther to risk challenging the law (4:10-16)?

_____

_____

_____

_____

4. Esther prayed, fasted, and physically prepared herself for the crisis ahead (4:16; sections C and D). What spiritual practices help you when facing something difficult or even unthinkable?

_____

_____

_____

_____

_____

5. What is celebrated in the Jewish feast of Purim (9:22-32; F:4-10)? Why is the story of Esther the centerpiece of this celebration?

_____

_____

_____

_____

_____

6. How did Queens Esther and Vashti each exemplify courage in the face of danger and indignity?

_____

_____

_____

_____

_____

7. Continuing the Conversation: By refusing to accommodate what she likely perceived as a degrading—even dangerous—summons from the king, Vashti loses her royal power but maintains her personal power. Have you ever had to make a choice that meant sacrificing some power or benefit for the sake of maintaining your dignity or autonomy? Or have you seen this occur in someone else's life? What was the end result?

_____

_____

_____

_____

_____

8. When you look back over your study of women in the Old Testament, what surprised you the most? What challenged you? What inspired you?

_____

_____

_____

_____

_____

9. If you had to select one woman's story from the Old Testament to tell young people as they grow up in our world and church today, whose story would it be? What message would you emphasize?

_____

_____

_____

_____

_____

CLOSING PRAYER

Prayer

"Who knows—perhaps it was for a time like this that you became queen?" (Esth 4:14)

In a time like this, O God, raise up in us a sense of purpose and justice. In our homes and workplaces, neighborhoods and churches, give us humility to be of service, courage to face harsh realities, and faithful companions who will keep our eyes fixed on you. We pray today for a greater awareness of what is happening around us and a deep knowledge of how you will work through us to help and inspire others. We lift up those who face injustice, and we pray for one another, especially . . .

ENDNOTES

1. King Asa of Judah "deposed his grandmother Maacah from her position as queen mother" because she had participated in the worship of Asherah (1 Kgs 15:13; cf. 14:21). The queen mother Athaliah reigns over Judah for six years (2 Kgs 11:3). The mother of King Jehoiachin of Judah is specifically named as one of the significant exiles in the first deportation to Babylon (2 Kgs 24:12, 15; Jer 29:2). Each of these women, like Bathsheba, is the mother of a younger son who succeeds to the throne rather than an elder brother (or uncle). In the northern kingdom (Israel) Jezebel is called "queen mother" (2 Kgs 10:13) and seems to have continued to wield influence during the reign of her son Joram (2 Kgs 9:22).

2. The phrase "knowledge of good and evil" is used in other biblical passages to describe children. The children who will be allowed to enter the land of promise are described as those "who as yet do not know good from evil" (Deut 1:39). The child who is a sign for Ahaz will not yet know "to reject evil and choose good" before the threat to Ahaz's kingdom is gone (Isa 7:15-16).

3. The wise woman of Tekoa says that David is like an angel of God, knowing good and bad (2 Sam 14:17).

4. Other terms used for this figure include Wisdom Woman, Lady Wisdom, and Dame Wisdom, although the latter two are less common now because of their monarchical connotations.

5. The Greek additions are numbered either as chapters A–F or as 10:4–16:24. This commentary follows the numbering of the New American Bible Revised Edition (chs. A–F).

BIBLIOGRAPHY

Bach, Alice, ed. *The Pleasure of Her Text: Feminist Readings of Biblical and Historical Texts*. Philadelphia: Trinity Press International, 1990.

Bellis, Alice O. *Helpmates, Harlots, Heroes: Women's Stories in the Hebrew Bible*. Louisville, KY: Westminster/John Knox, 1994.

Brenner, Athalya. *The Israelite Woman: Social Role and Literary Type in Biblical Narrative*. 2nd ed. London: Bloomsbury, 2015.

Darr, Kathryn Pfisterer. *Far More Precious Than Jewels: Perspectives on Biblical Women*. Gender and the Biblical Tradition. Louisville, KY: Westminster/John Knox, 1991.

Day, Peggy L., ed. *Gender and Difference in Ancient Israel*. Minneapolis: Fortress, 1989.

Gafney, Wilda C. M. *Daughters of Miriam: Women Prophets in Ancient Israel*. Minneapolis: Fortress, 2008.

LaCocque, André. *The Feminine Unconventional: Four Subversive Figures in Israel's Tradition*. Overtures to Biblical Theology. Minneapolis: Fortress, 1990.

McKenna, Megan. *Not Counting Women and Children: Neglected Stories from the Bible*. Maryknoll, NY: Orbis, 1994.

Meyers, Carol. *Rediscovering Eve: Ancient Israelite Women in Context*. Oxford: Oxford University Press, 2013.

Newsom, Carol A., Sharon H. Ringe, and Jacqueline E. Lapsley, eds. *The Women's Bible Commentary*. 3rd ed. Louisville, KY: Westminster/John Knox, 2012.

Nunnally-Cox, J. Ellen. *Foremothers: Women of the Bible*. San Francisco: Harper & Row, 1981.

O'Connor, Kathleen M. *The Wisdom Literature*. Message of Biblical Spirituality 5. Wilmington, DE: Michael Glazier, 1990.

Schüssler-Fiorenza, Elisabeth. *But She Said: Feminist Practices of Biblical Interpretation*. Boston: Beacon Press, 1992.

Sleevi, Mary Lou. *Women of the Word: Art and Story*. Notre Dame, IN: Ave Maria, 1989.

Trible, Phyllis. *God and the Rhetoric of Sexuality*. Overtures to Biblical Theology. Philadelphia: Fortress, 1978.

Trible, Phyllis. *Texts of Terror: Literary-Feminist Readings of Biblical Narratives*. Overtures to Biblical Theology. Minneapolis: Fortress, 2022.

Williams, Delores S. *Sisters in the Wilderness: The Challenge of Womanist God-Talk*. Maryknoll, NY: Orbis Books, 1993.

Winter, Miriam Therese. *WomanWisdom: A Feminist Lectionary and Psalter: Women of the Hebrew Scriptures: Part One*. New York: Crossroad, 1991.

Winter, Miriam Therese. *WomanWitness: A Feminist Lectionary and Psalter: Women of the Hebrew Scriptures: Part Two*. New York: Crossroad, 1991.

PRAYING WITH YOUR GROUP

Because we know that the Bible allows us to hear God's voice, prayer provides the context for our study and sharing. By speaking and listening to God and each other, the discussion often grows to more deeply bond us to one another and to God.

At *the beginning and end of each lesson* simple prayers are provided for individual use, and also may be used within the group setting. Most of the closing prayers provided with each lesson relate directly to a theme from that lesson and encourage you to pray together for people and events in your local community.

Of course, there are many ways to center ourselves in God's presence as we gather together in groups around the word of God. We provide some additional suggestions here knowing you and your group will make prayer a priority as part of your gathering. These are simply alternative ways to pray if your group would like to try something different from those prayers provided in the previous pages.

Conversational Prayer

This form of prayer allows for the group members to pray in their own words in a way that is not intimidating. The group leader begins with Step One, inviting all to focus on the presence of Christ among them. After a few moments of quiet, the group leader invites anyone in the group to voice a prayer or two of thanksgiving; once that is complete, then anyone who has personal intentions may pray in their own words for their needs; finally, the group prays for the needs of others.

A suggested process:
In your own words, speak simple and short prayers to allow time for others to add their voices.

Focus on one "step" at a time, not worrying about praying for everything in your mental list at once.

Step One	Visualize Christ. Welcome him. Imagine him present with you in your group. Allow time for some silence.
Step Two	Gratitude opens our hearts. Use simple words such as, "Thank you, Lord, for . . ."
Step Three	Pray for your own needs knowing that others will pray with you. Be specific and honest. Use "I" and "me" language.

Step Four	Pray for others by name, with love.
	You may voice your agreement ("Yes, Lord").
	End with gratitude for sharing concerns.

Praying Like Ignatius

St. Ignatius Loyola, whose life and ministry are the foundation of the Jesuit community, invites us to enter into Scripture texts in order to experience the scenes, especially scenes of the gospels or other narrative parts of Scripture. Simply put, this is a method of creatively imagining the scene, viewing it from the inside, and asking God to meet you there. Most often, this is a personal form of prayer, but in a group setting, some of its elements can be helpful if you allow time for this process.

A suggested process:

- Select a scene from the chapters in the particular lesson.

- Read that scene out loud in the group, followed by some quiet time.

- Ask group members to place themselves in the scene (as a character, or as an onlooker) so that they can imagine the emotions, responses, and thinking that may have taken place. Notice the details and the tone, and imagine the interaction with the Lord that is taking place.

- Share with the group any insights that came to you in this quiet imagining.

- Allow each person in the group to thank God for some insight and to pray about some request that may have surfaced.

Sacred Reading (or Lectio Divina)

This method of prayer invites us to "listen with the ear of the heart" as St. Benedict's rule would say. We listen to the words and the phrasing, asking God to speak to our innermost being. Again, this method of prayer is most often used in an individual setting but may also be used in an adapted way within a group.

A suggested process:

- Select a scene from the chapters in the particular lesson.

- Read the scene out loud in the group, perhaps two times.

- Ask group members to ponder a word or phrase that stands out to them.

- The group members could then simply speak the word or phrase as a kind of litany of what was meaningful for your group.

- Allow time for more silence to ponder the words that were heard, asking God to reveal to you what message you are meant to hear, how God is speaking to you.

- Follow up with spoken intentions at the close of this group time.

REFLECTING ON SCRIPTURE

Reading Scripture is an opportunity not simply to learn new information but to listen to God who loves you. Pray that the same Holy Spirit who guided the formation of Scripture will inspire you to correctly understand what you read, and empower you to make what you read a part of your life.

The inspired word of God contains layers of meaning. As you make your way through passages of Scripture, whether studying a book of the Bible or focusing on a biblical theme, you may find it helpful to ask yourself these four questions:

What does the Scripture passage say?
Read the passage slowly and reflectively. Become familiar with it. If the passage you are reading is a narrative, carefully observe the characters and the plot. Use your imagination to picture the scene or enter into it.

What does the Scripture passage mean?
Read the footnotes in your Bible and the commentary provided to help you understand what the sacred writers intended and what God wants to communicate by means of their words.

What does the Scripture passage mean to me?
Meditate on the passage. God's word is living and powerful. What is God saying to you? How does the Scripture passage apply to your life today?

What am I going to do about it?
Try to discover how God may be challenging you in this passage. An encounter with God contains a challenge to know God's will and follow it more closely in daily life. Ask the Holy Spirit to inspire not only your mind but your life with this living word.